How to Write a Winning College Application Essay

MICHAEL JAMES MASON

How to Write a Winning College Application Essay

Revised 4th Edition

THREE RIVERS PRESS

NEW YORK

Library of Congress Cataloging-in-Publication Data
Mason, Michael (Michael James)
    How to write a winning college application essay / Michael James
Mason.—Rev. 4th ed.
    Includes bibliographical references and index.
    1. College applications—United States. 2. Exposition (Rhetoric) 3.
Universities and colleges—United States—Admission. I. Title.
LB2351.52.U6 M29 2000
378.1'.616—dc21   00-037361
                                                                 CIP

ISBN 0-7615-2426-6

10 9 8 7

*This book is dedicated to my students, past and present.
Their hopes, dreams and energy are the brightest inspiration.
And to the memory of my mother, Minnie Guthrie Mason,
the most dedicated and talented teacher I have ever known.*

CONTENTS

AUTHOR'S NOTE TO THE FOURTH EDITION

SINCE THE PUBLICATION of the first three editions of *How to Write a Winning College Application Essay*, thousands of students across the nation have used this book in the process of writing their personal statements for college and graduate school. Their comments about the book, expressed during workshops and in letters, have been most gratifying. In nearly every instance, students tell me that the system that is taught in this book works. Certainly, this is the highest and most meaningful praise that can come from the people who actually use this book. At the same time, the students who expressed their satisfaction with this book also did the work that is outlined in the pages that follow. They understood, as do all the college applicants who actually use this book, that there is no shortcut to writing an essay you are proud to send to the colleges of your choice.

The reason behind the effectiveness of this book is an uncomplicated one. It was created to help students to actually *write* the essay, and not merely to present students with examples of what a good essay in a college application should look like. Hopefully, you will find that we understand your predicament. The book is purposely designed to be a practical manual born of the experience of real students and admissions officers, the people who write and read the essays in college applications.

When it came time for a third—and now a fourth—edition of this book, I was reminded of the Old West adage "If it ain't broke, don't fix it." In all three of the subsequent editions of the book, it has made sense to talk to my students about suggested changes they might have, since they use the book on a day-to-day basis when preparing their college applications in the early fall. They made a few suggestions, asking more for additions to the text than for actual changes, especially where the SAT essay is discussed. I appreciate their help very sincerely. Teachers and counselors also have been helpful with feedback, and the resulting additions to the book are also in response to some of their comments.

More than a decade has passed since I began conducting the College Essay Workshops and reading thousands of college application essays. Though some features of this process have changed, much has remained the same. Certainly, the importance of the essay has grown, and far more students are aware of the crucial value of this document in their campaign to "get into Lucky U." Seniors in high school "stress out" about the essay more than ever before, and there are a considerable number of private college counselors who claim to have the inside track on what a good essay should be. Every week someone writes a short article in an education journal or family magazine, outlining briefly what every successful application essay should deliver. I've had a great opportunity over the years to talk to thousands of students about the essays they are challenged to write. Their difficulties in approaching this problem have, for the most part, remained similar. The purpose of this book continues to address the really important matter at hand, which is how to approach the essay as a practical writing task. There's not only a job to be done here, but a right way and a wrong way to do it as well. Ultimately, the essay has essential qualities it must convey. If writing technique is followed correctly, a great essay written ten years ago could still be a great essay today.

The fourth edition of *How to Write a Winning College Application Essay* has changed in a variety of ways, without altering the basic philosophy of the first three editions. Information has been added to chapters to clarify important details previously requested by students. There are also updates to strategy outlines at the close of certain chapters to help students remember what they've read or give them a new way of thinking about this very unique writing challenge. Finally, in my experience with reading students' work, I've noticed some recurrent bad habits that have hurt otherwise good essays and I have added mention of them throughout the book.

Also in this edition, I've updated chapter 8—Under Pressure: The *SAT II: Writing Test*—to reflect student input from the SAT II workshops I've conducted and updated information I've gathered from friends at the College Board. Again, this chapter is designed to both inform you about what the essay test entails and help you score the maximum number of points on the exam. The results of the test essay will be "sharing quarters" in your application jacket with your application essay or personal statement. The quality of both examples of your writing prowess should have some "family resemblance," which is why we include a chapter devoted to the SAT II essay and continue to update it with each edition.

Anyone interested in contacting me regarding additional programs offered through the College Essay Workshop, such as our essay reading service, essay workshop information in your region of the country, and our essay counseling service, should send inquiries to the following e-mail address:
mmason@lmumail.lmu.edu

PREFACE

How to Write a Winning College Application Essay is the result of several years of writing workshops for students who wanted to write a good essay that would increase their chances of getting into the college of their choice. Students in the College Essay Workshop in Los Angeles expressed concern that they didn't know what to write about when they faced the prospect of the application essay. Some of these students have great GPAs and board scores, and some have average scores and "numbers" but marvelous potential to be excellent college students. They wanted to show themselves in the best light, but they didn't know how to make it happen.

No one will ever write a book that can guarantee acceptance into your dream college. Reading good essays that impressed admissions counselors won't make you a better writer, just as knowing the facts behind the college application won't turn your essay into a masterpiece. Only your ability to express yourself in honest, straightforward language will enable you to write a winning essay. This book can help you put your best image on paper. It will teach you to let the essay speak from your heart about what life means to you.

You don't have to be a star scholar or a superhero to write a great application essay. You just have to show on paper that you know some things about yourself and that your life has meaning and perspective. Slick, humorous essays, imaginative twists of plot, cute metaphors, and wild presentations have worked for hundreds of students, to be sure; but thousands of good students have been accepted into colleges of their choice because their essays were honest, moving, and sensitive. Their essays revealed their values, insights, and spirit. This book can help you find that special voice that says *this is me*. If you are serious about giving this part of the application your "best shot," then you have to do the work it will take to make it happen. Give yourself two full weeks to work on this project, two hours per night. That's right—two hours per night. Make it part of your schedule and put aside everything but these serious duties until you are finished and satisfied with the results. This essay, unlike everything else you've written before now, really counts. The only way you can lose in this situation is if you don't try to do your best. Your best will require effort. You can do that . . . and you know it.

ACKNOWLEDGMENTS

MANY PEOPLE WERE instrumental in bringing this book to fruition. My students during the last fifteen years in high schools in San Francisco and Los Angeles taught me what they needed to know—most especially the students at Marymount High School in West Los Angeles, where the College Essay Workshop began in 1986. I am especially indebted to: Sr. Colette McManus, R.S.H.M., for her support during the early years of the program; Sr. Celine Cripps, R.S.H.M., for her cheerful encouragement and confidence; and Dick Friedman for listening. A special thanks for teaching me about teaching must go to Renate Kerris, who was always aware of what education is supposed to provide students, and the gift that students give to teachers. Fr. Russ Roide, S.J., late of Stanford and now in San Francisco, who was the first to steer me on this path, deserves a heartfelt thanks, as does Sr. Justine Lyons, R.S.C.J., who will always be the quintessential educator in my eyes. Dr./Fr. Joe Burke was an inspirational friend and mentor throughout the writing of the first draft of this book and is one of America's "great teachers." A very special and personal thanks is extended to my friends and colleagues who believed in this book: Fr. Robert Walsh, S.J., president of Loyola High School of Los Angeles—a fine educator and a great friend; Bill Thomason, principal at Loyola High, for his enthusiasm, wit, and support of my work with students; Tom Goepel, for his wise counsel and wry humor; Erin Hoffman for her Irish wit and wisdom; Terry Caldwell, for his constant support and encouragement; Dr. Peter Wright, Lou Ann Berardi, Sylvia Rousseve, Edwina Lynch, Mary Arney and Jerry Lindner, S.J.—masters in the teaching arts; the faculty at Loyola High—educators extraordinaire; Dr. Candace Poindexter, for her exuberance and insight into teaching young people to write; admissions counselors Joyce Bryson, Gail Devine, Pepper McCulloch, and Diane Sheffield, for their support and faith; Mike Dennison, Tom Vavra, Tom Gallagher, Geoff Joy, and Tim Haley, for backing the program; my students at Loyola High School, whose spirit and heart are always with me; Chris Zavoli of the College Board, for her kind help on each edition with information on the *SAT II: Writing Test;* Joe Borda, who knew the value of the College Essay Workshop and kept it alive; the late Vida Sidrys, a loving teacher who never doubted; Brian and Vic at Kanecko Metzgar Design; David Hoffman for pointing the way; Sr. Gregory Naddy, R.S.H.M., at Marymount College; Dean Jim Reeves for his faith and wisdom; Dean Ellen Richmond at Columbia University for her enthusiastic help with admissions information; Don Marino, John Pierce, Paul Eastup, and Dr. Joe Cuseo at Marymount College, for the laughter in the storm; Sandra Ross, Michelle Pierce and the late Jules Teissere—three marvelous teachers of writing—and Sharon Johnson at the Learning Center. The students of Marymount College and Loyola Marymount University will always have my affectionate thanks for their kindness and cheerful dedication to words and ideas. The Reins family—Monte, Madeline, Janelle, and Jen—have my grateful love for letting an Irish kid be part of such a fine "bella familia." To my son, Kevin, for his beautiful little boy ideas and his big angel smile, and to my daughter, Kaelin, for the inspiration of sparkling baby girl eyes, go my joyful thanks. And my loving gratitude goes to my darling wife, Jacqueline Reins Mason, the admissions officer I fell in love with who helped me in ways beyond words. A final note of sincere thanks and admiration must go to all of the admissions officers in the country who gave so selflessly of their time in the making of this book. A labor of love, it surely was.

1

What's It All About?

The college application process is not fun. Anyone who has had to apply to college in the last twenty-five years has experienced a very complex and expensive undertaking that guarantees nothing, promises less, and is filled with mystery and stress. For many high school seniors and two-year college sophomores, organizing and completing college applications is a very unpleasant experience. Your college counselors have told you where you may have the best chance of "getting in" based on your SAT scores, grades, and class rank. Dreams can take a real beating when you find out that no matter how well you've done with the "numbers," there is still a chance you won't be accepted to "Lucky U." because thousands of other students are also trying to get into next year's class.

In your quest to "get in" to your dream college, nothing is in the bag. You must do your absolute best to show every facet of your ability and potential to the college admissions committee, pull whatever strings you may have, and make sure that you have one or more backup schools to attend if "Lucky U." doesn't have room for you. Doing your best to deliver a strong application will allow you the peace of mind that comes from knowing you made every possible effort to show the admissions officers who you are and what kind of student you are and will be. If you think that your "numbers" (the statistics that compute your past performance such as board scores and GPA) are all that really count and if you're prepared to rest on your laurels, then you will not do your best in the application process.

The application process reaches beyond statistics to reveal several intangibles about you that can't be covered by the numbers. Recommendations from your counselors and teachers are part of the equation that will determine your "acceptability." Your work experiences and extracurricular activities have some impact on the image you present to the admissions team. If you get an interview at "Lucky U." and present yourself well, this can have a positive effect on your chances for admission. Finally, there is the college application essay, a written example of how your brain communicates what you think and feel. The essay also fills in the gray areas in your application file that can't be determined by scores and letter grades. All of these ingredients in the menu of college application procedures are extremely important. They plead your case with expert testimony, substantiated facts, and personal presence. If you liken the college application process to preparing a case before a jury of admissions officers, you can understand why good lawyers use every element of evidence to persuade the jury that the cause is just and true. Every detail counts. Each scrap of evidence is valuable. The client's future is on the line, and nothing of importance should be taken lightly or ignored. Although you're not exactly on trial when you apply for a position in a college's graduation class, you certainly are pleading a case that demands care and intelligent attention. You won't do time in the strict sense, if your case fails, but doing four years at the College from Hell just because you didn't do your best to plead your case is not a happy prospect. Being rejected at "Lucky U." after completing a spectacular application that you were proud to send is far better than getting the rejection letter from your dream school, knowing that you could have done better.

The grades are in and the SATs are over. You have lined up your recommendations and have your "brag sheet," the history of your activities and accomplishments, outlined and ready to use in the application. Perhaps you've set up an interview if the college of your choice offers that opportunity. Now you have to write an essay, or personal statement. The application may ask you simply to "Tell us about yourself, including any information that may be helpful to the admissions committee in determining your readiness for college life." Your applications may include a request for a "Personal Statement" and nothing more. Some of your applications may call for you to choose from three different topics, such as: (1) If you could spend a day with any historical figure, who would it be and how would you spend the time you have with that person? (2) In the event of a natural disaster which three things would you want to have with you to survive? (3) Write page 312 of your autobiography. Essay topics such as these are common in most college applications. They are meant to reveal certain facets of you to the admissions committee. The college application is not merely a writing sample that proves you can spell or write a complete sentence. The written responses that you give to the essay assignment in your application are your golden opportunity to show the admissions committee a special side of yourself. They are your chance to live and breathe in the application.

Don't Panic!

PANIC IS a common reaction when faced with writing a college application essay. It should be. At first it seems that whatever 500 words (or fewer) you write will never say what you think they should. You ask yourself, Where do I start? What do the admissions officers think when they read these essays? Do I have to write a Work of Art? Do I have to be funny? I haven't done anything that I can write about in an essay that will impress anyone. Do I brag about my GPA? HELP!!!!!

The Objective

THE BEST way to get control of yourself and the essay is to calm down. This college application essay is a writing assignment unlike any other that you've had to write. It is not a high school composition. This essay has consequences. It also has an objective. A good starting point for getting control of this writing project is to determine the objective of the essay.

> A good starting point for getting control of this writing project is to determine the objective of the essay.

Every college admissions officer to whom I've spoken

about the application essay says that the essay is intended to help the committee get a sense of the person who is applying to their college. What is your objective then? It is to communicate a sense of who you are. Simply stated, *the essay is you.*

There is a good chance that in the course of the last year you've read articles about the college application essay in magazines, newspapers, and information handouts at your high school or junior college. You've also seen a few successful or unique college application essays that were written by other students. The advice about the essay that appears in print every year is usually the same. It's good advice, too. Often it includes the following:

- Write clearly and with good grammar.
- Be yourself.
- Don't write too much about too many things.
- Read essays that have proved successful.

Unfortunately, even good advice is not enough to help you write a good, solid application essay. This book is designed to help you to develop a method, a technique for writing the essay that conveys a positive image of *you.*

The Method

THERE IS a technique that all writers use when faced with an assignment that asks them to communicate to a specific audience. It's basic and includes three distinct steps: research, development, and execution. The college application essay is a writing assignment with a specific audience. If you are going to communicate to that audience, you should know who those people are, what they look for when they read, the criteria they use to judge the work, and what is important to them as professionals and human beings. To ignore your audience and just write whatever you feel like writing can be a disastrous mistake. The first step in your research phase of writing should be to answer the question: Who is the audience? Chapter 2 of this book, "The Admissions Officers Speak!" is intended to give you a sense of your audience in their own words.

It gives you a solid picture of the real people who are going to read your essay. Of course, every person is unique and differs in taste and attitude. Admissions officers are people just like you. They are, however, professionals with standards and, as such, share a similar perspective on the essay portion of the application.

> Admissions officers are people just like you. They are, however, professionals with standards and, as such, share a similar perspective on the essay portion of the application.

Before you jump to chapter 2, there is another aspect of research that bears mention. The college of your choice has spent considerable money to produce a viewbook or catalog to reveal to prospective applicants the features that the college offers its students. It is a very enlightening document if read and studied with some intelligence. Don't write a word until you take a serious look at the viewbook for each of the colleges to which you will apply. Why? The college viewbook is the admissions office's marketing statement for the college. Between the glossy covers of the viewbook are the words and ideas that the college uses to communicate its image and principles. What do the pictures in the viewbook communicate to you? What is the college trying to tell you about itself in these pictures? Are the pictures filled with images of tradition? Is college community and active campus life highlighted often? Are the library and research played up heavily? Is the surrounding urban setting a key feature in the college's self-image?

The words in the college viewbook are also a declaration of the values that the college holds dear. The following excerpt from the Barnard College viewbook is loaded with buzzwords that appear in most college marketing publications. It should give you a sense of what the college thinks are prominent concepts—ideas that it wants its students to share as part of the campus community:

Barnard presents its students with a unique combination for undergraduate study: the intimacy of a small women's liberal arts college, access to the vast academic resources of Columbia University, and the opportunity to take advantage of the unparalleled offerings of New York City.

President Ellen V. Futter has said that "the liberal arts should be liberating in every sense, freeing you from preconceptions, enlarging your appreciation of the world around you, and extending your options for the future. The Barnard experience is not merely preparation for life but life itself—in the timeless, exhilarating, and comfortable environment that can perhaps only be found in a small women's college."

Barnard's special world encompasses coeducational experience through the academic, extracurricular, and social opportunities open to students in a university college. High standards of scholarship and a special concern for the education of women make the pursuit of a Barnard education truly distinctive.

This excerpt gives anyone who reads it a clear idea about what the college cherishes and looks for in its prospective students. The buzzwords in this and any viewbook can give you a feeling for the qualities for which the admissions committees are looking in the candidates who apply. Circle the words in the preceding passage that you think are indicative of what is important to these people. Do the same thing in the viewbooks of all the colleges to which you're applying. They're telling you who they are and what they think. Put this information in writing and see if your essay appeals to these ideas and values when you're in the writing phase.

An additional document published by the college admissions committee that reveals some insights into their criteria for acceptance is the teacher's evaluation form in the application. The typical evaluation form asks the teacher to rate you and discuss you in some of the following terms: intellectual purpose, motivation, relative maturity, integrity, independence, originality, initiative, leadership potential, capacity for growth, special talents, and enthusiasm. If you really want to know what the admissions committee is interested in seeing in your essay, this list of typical evaluation criteria gives a fairly clear indication. Take a look at the teacher's evaluation form for each of the colleges to which you plan to apply and make a photocopy for your research purposes. Pull out your dictionary and write the definitions of all these terms so you have a clear idea of what is important to your audience before you begin to think of a topic or a direction.

When your research on the audience is complete, the next step in the method outlined in this book is to do some research on *you*. Chapter 3, "The History of You, Part One," gives you a technique for compiling a wide variety of personal information about yourself that you may not realize you have. Do each of the exercises in chapter 3 (not just the ones that you think are fun or easy). Every piece of evidence is important in this case. The smallest, seemingly most insignificant fragment might be useful in presenting who you are. Don't take shortcuts. You're the client. Be good to yourself and do a thorough research job.

The second phase of the method offered in this book appears in chapters 4 and 5, "Go to Commercial" and "Do's and Don'ts." When your research from chapters 2 and 3 is complete, it is time to decide on the attitude or mind-set you must maintain as you begin to write. "Go to Commercial" explains some techniques that may be helpful to you in visualizing the essay as an appeal to the market. You're the product and the admissions committees are the market. The essay isn't a hard-sell advertisement, but it is intended to market you to the college. You should be aware of approaches that work and those that are less favorable. "Do's and Don'ts," on the other hand, is a chapter that

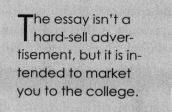

The essay isn't a hard-sell advertisement, but it is intended to market you to the college.

gives you practical guidance on both solid technique and everything you should be careful to avoid doing in the essay.

The execution phase outlined in this book appears in chapter 6, "It's Showtime!" At this point, you are ready to write. Chapter 6 is a step-by-step approach to writing the essay. It discusses writing techniques that will give your work some design and purpose. You have already studied in writing classes some of the style and composition elements covered in this chapter, but here these techniques are given a perspective that applies to the college application essay and will help you control your delivery and critique your copy. Keep in mind that the college application essay is not a high school composition but rather a special kind of communication about who you really are.

Before you write your final draft read chapter 7, "The Good, the Bad, and the Ugly." This chapter offers examples of good essays and mediocre essays. Though terrific essays are somewhat valuable, there is more to be learned from essays that don't work because they afford us a clear picture of what to avoid. Most admissions people agree that 75 percent of the essays they read are mediocre and another 10 percent are downright poor. If your essay looks like one of these "bad" essays, then you have the opportunity to change your style before you send it off to "Lucky U." Brief comments accompany each sample essay.

Those of you who are applying to graduate schools will find chapter 9 helpful for its discussion of letters of intent. My suggestion is that you follow all the steps in each chapter of this book after you read "The Graduate School Essay."

"Final Touches," the last chapter in this book, is a checklist that you should use *before* you send your essay to the college admissions office. It covers important points of form and content in the essay that are mentioned in various chapters throughout this book. It is a quick refresher course that reviews a few of the fundamentals you want to remember at mailing time. If you follow the guidelines in chapter 11, you might avoid an inadvertent error that could hurt your essay's effectiveness. Like any good pilot, you want to check your vehicle for safety's sake . . . before you take off.

2

The Admissions Officers Speak!

Admissions officers are not robots or monsters. Nor are they obsessed with statistics. They don't believe everything they hear or read, and they went to high school once, just like you. Admissions officers are people. Many of them are fascinating and remarkably dedicated individuals. All have a tough job to do. Each year they have to create a freshman class for their college that will be bright, qualified, diverse, energetic, and durable enough to make it through to graduation four years later.

Recently I have spoken to many admissions officers from colleges all across the United States and asked them questions about the college application essay. Rather than summarize what they said to me, I decided to let you read some of their comments, quoted directly from the interviews. Here's what they had to say.

Question: How Important Is the Application Essay?

+ "An essay that is only average in quality would probably not undo a candidate's chances for admission. But an average essay or a poorly composed essay or one that looks like it was given all of ten minutes and written in pencil would certainly hurt the candidate's chances for admission. Not only could it damage a marginal candidate, but I think it would hurt a candidate well into the admissible range on the basis of more objective criteria."

+ "After the general information that is reported on the first form of our application—student activities, where they went to school, and that sort of thing—the first thing we read is the essay. It plays a very important part in terms of setting the tone for the rest of the application. It's kind of where we start to evaluate the student in our own mind; then we read through the rest of the application and look either for things to support our favorable impressions or things to turn around any negative impressions we got from the essay. If the student did interview, it's really the only other chance the student has to speak directly to us. Anything else is coming from their counselors, teachers, grades, transcripts, or whatever. It's really the personal part of the application."

+ "In our experience the college essay is very important. We use the essay to judge a person's writing ability, his or her ability to communicate thoughts in writing . . . to get a sense of who the person is and what he or she is looking for in an educational experience and what the person's previous educational experience has been like. We use the essay to get to know the person."

+ "The essay does make a big difference. For schools that don't require interviews, what you've got to show are your test scores, your GPA, activities, and your essay. Your essay is your one shot at communicating who you are and why someone should admit you to your chosen university. Even for schools that do require interviews, it sets the stage for that interview. It's very important."

> "Your essay is your one shot at communicating who you are and why someone should admit you to your chosen university."

✦ "There were many times that we would overrule the numbers and say 'Let's give this person a shot' based on our sense of the person and our belief that he or she was going to succeed because it came out of the essay and it came out of our interview."

✦ "No one's going to be admitted on the basis of an essay alone. The more competitive the institution is in terms of gaining admission, the more probable the essay will have greater importance in the admissibility of students, because we take only one out of every five students and everything's going to count on the application. The most important variable is going to be academic performance. Let's just say that when everything else is very comparable from one candidate to the next, the essay is really going to make a difference. We never look at the essay out of context, so it usually confirms the other information in the application; if it doesn't, then we're maybe skeptical. If somebody puts no effort into the essay, then certainly it will make a difference. In other words, if somebody puts something together in the 24 hours before they have to send it in and they do a slapdash job with the essay, certainly that can be held against the student. In some ways the essay can be damning in that if somebody has the credentials and everything else looks pretty solid but does a really poor job with the essay, we wonder how serious that person is about applying to this college; it could be the reason why somebody is not admitted."

Question: What Do You Look for in the Essay?

✦ "The basic nature of the essay is to check a student's writing style, the use of language, and the organization of thoughts in his or her statement. We look for something about his or her values, traumatic experiences or dramatic experiences, things that have impacted them. I think I like to read about the personal sensitivity that a student might have. Personal experiences and relationships are all important elements of a good essay. I also feel that the essay should not be just simply a regurgitation of information that's already in a student's résumé and already listed under activities and honors—things that are already presented in list form in some other part of the application. I also like to see students walk out on thin ice and use humor if it's natural for them to use humor, creativity, or cleverness. If it's not natural, then they shouldn't try that. I think, too, they need to write it in their own words. They shouldn't put on some kind of corporate vocabulary simply to try to impress the committee. We're more interested in personal style and the substance of the writing rather than how they can impress us with their vocabulary and their sentence structure."

> "I think I like to read about the personal sensitivity that a student might have."

✦ "I don't think everybody has to have some major event that they have to write about in their lives. I think the student has to use some creative juices to come up with an interesting way of talking about the family dog or a relationship with a sick aunt. Those are the kinds we like to read, those that aren't the typical "300 words, Pikes Peak out-the-rear-window-of-a-car essay."

✦ "We want essays that come straight from the heart. That's the point of the essay. Why do you want me? Why do you want me as a student on your campus? What are you going to contribute? I don't mean by being president of the senior class or being an All-American. There are lots of ways that students can contribute. They need to have a sense of themselves in order to present that in written form."

✦ "I'm looking for something that tells me about the person who's writing the essay. Sometimes that's revealed in the actual content of the essay and sometimes, more interestingly, in the way that the essay is written. A student's writing style can sometimes tell us as much about the student as the actual story itself. I like reading something interesting that's happened to students. The essays that I dread reading are, of course, the ones that start out about 'My trip to Europe' or something like that. If they do have a story to tell and it is something about their trip to Europe, I'd rather hear something about a specific incident that happened rather than a travelogue and summation that says, 'Now I have a greater understanding of the culture.' I also look for a certain degree of mechanics. I like to see things that are written concisely and clearly. I dread the long, long, long essay that brings in every unimportant detail about what they're trying to get across. I really like it when people can express themselves in a brief manner and also be effective at the same time. Also, I'm looking for people writing as they would speak. They're not really stretching themselves in terms of vocabulary, trying to impress the person with words they don't normally use or understand. They should speak honestly."

> "The essay is the part of the application over which the students have the most control."

✦ "Many people bomb when they try to be humorous because people's senses of humor don't always match. Someone may think something's funny, and it may be derogatory to someone else."

✦ "Obviously, there are people who have not put much time and effort into the essay; they're resting on the laurels of their good grades and high SATs or whatever, and that can certainly hurt them. Like I said, there's no one part of the application that's going to get them in or exclude them, so they really do have to spend time on the essay."

✦ "There are a lot of things we dislike reading—the things we dislike most are bland personality lists. Think of us hoping that the application will at least figuratively come alive in front of us, so when we're struggling to read applications at 10:30 P.M. on any given night, seven nights a week during the reading period, we're looking for a personality. We're looking to grasp hold of an individual. The essay is the part of the application over which the students have the most control. The essays we dislike the most are those that seemingly could have been written by 2,000 or 3,000 other applicants. An essay like this could just be plugged into this applicant, and it wouldn't reveal anything new about the candidate. We're looking for distinctiveness. We're looking for something that will distinguish this applicant from anyone else in the applicant pool or anyone else in that person's AP English class or senior year, whatever it may be."

✦ "It's important to communicate who you are. If I don't get a very good sense of the person, then I'm not very pleased with reading that essay. I interviewed a student who was not accepted to the college; this person used humor throughout his essay, and it came off really poorly. He tried to be funny. I didn't find him very humorous. He needed some time to grow up and mature before he came to college. What I've always looked for in a personal statement are people—who they are, how they understand themselves, and what their needs are—and beyond that, what they're looking for from the college and what some of their goals might be."

Question: What Advice Would You Give Students About the Essay?

✦ "If students use a word processor and if they write the same essay to more than one school, they should be darn sure they change the variable codes because the last thing a Dean of Admissions wants to hear is how badly a student wants to go to their competition across town. It happens all the time, believe me."

✦ "What I think we're all interested in is finding out if the applicant really understands the college. I think we each feel we have something special to offer students and there's a special character and various unique attributes that a college has. And when I say 'nice' attributes I don't mean nice buildings, or high-average SATs, or a high ranking or attractive location. Those things are very obvious. We're not looking for people to spout those things back to us. It's important for us to know that this student really understands what's special about the particular college to which he or she is applying, so my advice is to do your homework. Really talk to people about the college—current students, alumni, admissions counselors—to whomever you can gain access so that you can really discover this deep, underlying feeling that represents the college. We give the answer to that particular question right there in the viewbook. It's going to be in there, among other things. The overall character of the place is certainly going to be expressed in the viewbook—but go beyond that. Talk to as many people as you can and get opinions about the college from as many different resources as possible."

✦ "Most important, the essay should reflect a sense of self. That can often get lost. I don't know how many times I've met with students who were in the process of writing their essays and what I found again and again were people who were just hung up on writing the essay. They were sort of frozen. Here were these judges out there that they didn't know, admissions officers who were going to make an important judgment about their future. The students wanted to communicate the right things to those people, but they were just frozen and unable to really communicate who they were. So what I would repeatedly tell people is *'Relax, communicate who you are, and things will probably work out fine.'* Your best shot is to communicate to these people *who you are as a person.*"

✦ "There are some students who are reluctant to really open themselves up to other people. They don't want to say too much or tell too much to a stranger about who they are and what they've been through. But from my perspective I think it's helpful to do that. If you can really deal with some of the things you've gone through in your life in your essay, it can say a lot. One of the questions that we had on our application form had to do with previous educational experience: Please describe a positive or negative experience. Frequently we would

> "**I**t's important for us to know that this student really understands what's special about the particular college to which he or she is applying, so my advice is to do your homework."

hear students describe a not-so-positive experience. It was how they dealt with that experience that made the difference."

✦ "If you're not sincere, then it can be a real problem for you. All it takes is a phone call to the school. We've followed up on applications before, found out that something doesn't fit, and the student has been caught. So it's very important to be honest."

✦ "*Relax and communicate the real you.* If you put too much effort in trying to impress, I don't think it comes across well. You end up compromising yourself; you're trying to impress someone, and nine out of ten times it just doesn't work. If you focus on who you are and what you're hoping to get out of your college experience—be very sincere and honest about that—then I think your chances of success will be much greater."

✦ "The advice I generally give students is that they should be specific and concrete in their essays, but there is no type of essay that is necessarily better than another. Everyone's unique and different from the next person, and the way to get to that is to try to be as specific as possible. What we don't like to read are glittering generalities that really don't distinguish the applicant from anyone else. The more specific and the more revealing students are, the better the essay will be for us to read. It will be more interesting. It will be more vital."

✦ "I think one of the things that makes the whole process uncomfortable for a lot of kids is that probably for the first time in their lives they have to be self-reflective. Speaking directly to students I'd say, 'You have to stand back and be somewhat philosophical. It's not like answering a question on a history exam that's multiple choice. You really have to reflect.' I'd give students 'before-and-after' advice. The 'before' advice is to sit back and think of the essay as something more than just writing an essay for a college but rather a process of thinking about who you are. You're on the verge of making a commitment to

> "Take a step back and think about who you are and what makes you distinctive or different from the next person."

a college or university and maybe even going away to a college that may have a significant impact on your life. Take a step back and think about who you are and what makes you distinctive or different from the next person. It could be an interest in your life. It could be an incident in your life. It could be a variety of different things. I would advise students to look at it that way. Then after you've written your essay, put it aside for at least 48 hours and then come back to it and read it. Try to read it as objectively as you can and then ask yourself whether or not you think this essay is distinctively 'you'? Does this essay reflect what is unique about you compared to the people in your senior class and other people applying to college? If it isn't, or you know that somebody else could have written this essay—Johnnie Jones who sits three seats down to the left of you in your English class—then it's not good enough because it doesn't truly reflect who you are. Write it again until it reflects you."

3

The History of You, Part One

How to Build a Strong Personal Information Profile . . . and What to Do with It

By now you have an idea of what the college essay is and what the people who read the essay think. The most important thing to remember, as you begin the writing portion of this program, is that the essay is supposed to be *personal.* This means that it's about *you.* If the essay's driving force and vital center is not *you,* then the essay can't do the job that it is intended to do.

O.K., so who *are* you? Your philosophy and history teachers have probably discussed the philosophical aspects of this question at one time or another in your classes over the past few years. Possibly this question is already exhausting you. It should. *Who am I?* is one of the toughest questions for most people of any age. Instead of looking at the question as a *problem* of philosophy, let's look at the question from a safe distance and then zoom in, as a

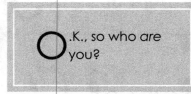

O.K., so who *are* you?

zoom in, as a camera would if it were telling a story about you in pictures.

If you could take a camera crew back to the day you were born and shoot the entire story of you, you would have amassed a large amount of material by now. That material could be edited down to a program about you. It wouldn't be a philosophical story about you, but it would give people a decent picture of the events, individuals, and forces that helped form your *personal* story.

There's an old saying in Broadway theater: "You're only as good as your material. . . ." For any story to be effective, you should always get as much background material as possible before you put the story together. This way you can choose the really strong scenes from a large volume of possible choices. That camera crew that you might bring along in your life, if you could, would need to shoot details, record interviews, and pick up random thoughts and conversations. It would aim for events that were turning points, not just your graduation from grammar school or your first day in kindergarten. The things that help make any story solid are both great and small, so all kinds of meaningful moments should be considered. Often the little things count the most.

Now you may react to this in one of two ways. Either you think, "Jeez, my story would be so boring. Who'd want to watch it?" or "Brother, if I tell them about *that,* they'll never let me into college anywhere!" The fact is, however, that you do have an incredible story to tell. And like most college-bound high school students, you can learn how to capture the material that's waiting right there inside you. That's the first step: gather the material. You have to collect as much information as you can find about yourself from as many sources as there are at your disposal. You are about to go on a rather creative scavenger hunt.

The Hunt

Gathering the Material

Whenever film editors begin putting a movie together for the producers and director, the first thing they do is look at all the raw footage that has been shot. Everything is screened, and each scene and "take" is viewed by the editors so they can begin to get a feel for the material. They've read the script—this is especially true in documentary films about real people and events—and though the film may read well on paper, if the written material is not captured on film it can't be used in the movie. Common sense, right? This very same approach—getting as much on film as possible to give the editor something to work with—is an effective strategy that will help make your college essay a pleasure to read for its coverage of you. *Coverage* is the key word and is fairly self-explanatory. You are the topic of the story and you have to be covered from several different angles before you start to write a single sentence of the essay itself.

In preparing to write the college essay, *information* is *power*. No matter what the essay topic may be, you will need information. The more that you know about yourself, the more confident you will be about the choices you make when you write about yourself.

> The more that you know about yourself, the more confident you will be about the choices you make when you write about yourself.

PERSONAL PROFILE

1. Who are the five people who have most influenced you?

2. What do you read?

3. List three virtues that you admire and respect.

4. Discuss three significant lessons you have learned.

5. Tell us about three memorable experiences you have had.

6. Discuss a failure that taught you something.

7. Respond to three quotes that mean something to you.

8. Remember your greatest success.

9. Name five things that you know.

10. Discuss your definition of happiness.

11. What do your parents remember about you?

12. What are your earliest memories?

13. What is an education supposed to provide?

Many high school students whom I've taught have spent so much time trying to fit in or be like other people that they have no sense of their own unique qualities. You all know someone who's afraid of being called "weird" or who thinks that anything that isn't trendy is "strange." Those people write terrible college essays. They write only about experiences that are supposedly acceptable—such as their yearbook experiences, or being on a team, or their trips to Europe. Their information about them-

14. List and describe five special things about you.

15. What is your "one-sentence philosophy of life"?

16. What is the funniest thing that ever happened to you?

17. What makes the world go round?

18. Picture the five places you've been that impressed you the most.

19. What is your favorite social activity?

20. What is your favorite intellectual or artistic activity?

21. Describe yourself to a stranger.

22. Tell the story of a fear you conquered.

23. Discuss three goals that you have in life.

24. List ten things you like and ten things you don't like at all.

25. What do your friends say that they like most about you?

26. What question have you always wanted answered and why?

selves is so limited that their choices for writing the essay are common and limited, too.

The first thing to keep in mind is that high school is not the only thing that has formed you as a person. You have a big life ahead of you, that's for sure, but you also have another big life behind you—the one that got you here. In "The Story of Your Life, Part One," momentous events and discoveries have occurred. In order for you to tell us any significant story about that life and the person in it, you'll need to do some coverage *before* you edit the piece. Where do you start?

There are three steps in putting information on paper for the college essay: self-reflection, interview, and research. The following list of activities is an important part of your college essay preparation and uses all three of these techniques to collect information. These are activities that you should do quickly, while the desire to write a good essay is greatest. (Don't take more than three days to fill out the profile list that follows or you'll lose momentum.)

Carefully read the Personal Profile list on pages 24–25 before you tackle any of the individual activities. My experience with students in the College Essay Workshops in Los Angeles has been that people who do each exercise in the order given benefit most from the program. Each activity is designed to work with other exercises, so skipping around and doing only the ones that look easy or fun will limit your possibilities. After you've read the list through, go on to the explanations for each individual activity.

Once you've read the list a few times and thought about some of the activities, get some writing paper, a pen, and a pencil. Find a quiet place to work, somewhere that will allow you to think. (The library is a good choice.)

> Our ability to appreciate inspirational people says much about who we are.

The most important aspect of writing is the thinking that you do before you start to write. Do not rush that part of the process or you will get off to a poor start. The Personal Profile demands some different kinds of thinking from you, but you'll be using your memory first. Take notes on the paper in front of you as you move through each item on the list. Write everything or anything that comes to mind as you go along. Use at least one sheet of paper for each number on the list. Relax, take a deep breath . . . let's start.

1. Who Are the Five People Who Have Most Influenced You?

INSPIRATION IS like magic that can transform us and lift our spirits. We all need to be inspired in some way to achieve our goals and live up to our dreams. Inspiration is a force that can fuel us with extra energy to push onward when life becomes rough; it is the spark that ignites belief in ourselves and lights the way when obstacles stand between us and our objectives. Inspiration is a precious gift given by people to one another. Our ability to appreciate inspirational people says much about who we are. The college application essay lends itself well to brief mention of inspirational people. From the time we are born and throughout the rest of our lives, we are influenced by many people. Their words, work, behavior, and achievements, whether we know them personally or admire them from afar, can make a difference in our lives. Parents, friends, historical figures, strangers we meet by chance, even fictional characters in novels who have been brought to life on the page can exert significant influence on the way we live and the decisions we make. A discussion of an individual whom you respect and admire can reveal tremendous insight into your character for an admissions committee. Of course, a list of people who have influenced you is useless without an explanation of what exactly it is about them that has inspired you.

Sometimes it's difficult to begin to write about yourself. It can create a kind of self-conscious block that allows you to see only close-ups and obscures the important people, events, and experiences around you that also are part of your picture. One

way to ease into the topic of you is to write about how someone else has inspired you to become the person you are. This
kind of approach can be used to open your essay, a kind of
kickoff point that can lead to many other topics in later paragraphs. Whether you later choose to mention a person you admire, you still need to write something down now. It will help
start you thinking about yourself in ways that can be trans-
ferred later to the essay, and it will pull you out of that groove
of "talking about myself" that makes the essay an unpleasant
experience for so many students.

Is this an exercise about heroes and heroines? Not necessarily. If you have heroes you admire, they certainly deserve to
be discussed in this section. But the people who inspired you
may be living or dead, real or fictional. It doesn't matter what
label we use to identify them. Hero, mentor, or role model,
they've made a difference in your life and that's important.
Who are they? What qualities do they have that inspire you?
Did they ever say or do something that moved you to emulate
them in some way? Perhaps they are people who strike you as
heroic and admirable, despite the fact that they are unknown
and unsung. Perhaps you have been moved by someone's
ability to handle his or her circumstances. You may admire
a person's strength in the face of adversity or his or her behavior when "the chips were down." All these people qualify as
inspirational.

Some students have used a brief mention of inspirational
people with great success. One young woman wrote very
thoughtfully about her younger brother, whose cheerfulness
and strength as he faced a frightening illness became her inspiration to appreciate the value of every moment. Another senior
discussed her admiration for Queen Elizabeth I, in praise of
her success in a man's world despite the sexism of the
Renaissance and Raleigh. A young man in one of my workshops began his essay with a hilarious tribute to Bugs Bunny,

in appreciation of the rabbit's ability to suffer a fool with fi-
nesse. The reasons *why* you are influenced or inspired by someone are far more revealing of your character than the person
you choose.

Though you might think twice before electing The Toxic
Avenger as an inspiration for your life, you should try to think
about everyone you've known or met—or those you'd like to
meet—who have had a positive influence on you in some way.
Characters you read about in literature or see in films are legitimate influences, too. It's your list. Anyone you admire should
be included.

2. What Do You Read?

THIS ISN'T a test question. Think about it. What have you
been reading? Try to list several books, especially those you've
been reading for enjoyment. Leave textbooks and assigned
reading off your list at the beginning and put them at the bottom of your list when you've exhausted every other avenue.
Include magazines you like and even comic books. Trash reading is acceptable, too. It's your list, so fill it with what you really read . . . not with books you think will impress the
admissions people. You are just collecting information here
and may use some or none of it later when you start to write
your essay.

Take a few minutes to record anything that you have read
in the last year. Now, what's your favorite book of all time?
Write down why you like it so much. Look at the books on
your list and pick the three that are the most meaningful to
you. Write the author's name for each one and describe what
you find most interesting or compelling about each book.
What literary characters in these books interested you the
most? Explain why you are drawn to those characters. Do any

of them remind you of yourself? Write it down. Do they remind you of anyone you know? Write it down. Why did you read these books? What thoughts came from reading these books? Any reflections or comments you have on any books you've read? If reading is important to you, jot down some reasons why you like to read.

3. List Three Virtues That You Admire and Respect

WHAT IS a virtue? Students who have taken my course on the college essay often ask me this question. Bravery, trust, dedication, and charity are virtues that are common to many of our respected heroes in life. Love, hope, and faith are virtues that everyone can use to handle the difficulties in life, but there are many other kinds of virtue. The dictionary definition for virtue is "Conformity to a standard of right . . . a moral excellence; a beneficial quality or power of a thing." Virtues bring meaning and direction to life. Most heroes and heroines, for example, adhere to certain rules of behavior and demonstrate virtuous qualities that set them apart from other people.

> Virtues are the foundations of your character and can paint a very clear picture of the special kind of individual you are.

Why should virtue be an important consideration when you prepare to write your college essay? Any person of character should be able to demonstrate a sense of morality. Everyone has some moral code to use in order to direct choices and behavior. Virtues are what make up your moral code. They help you make decisions. When you think about the "right" thing to do, your virtues lend an important influence to your final actions. They are the foundations of your character and can paint a very clear picture of the special kind of individual you are.

College admissions officers are very interested in *who* you are, beyond your statistics and brag sheets. Your character, your virtues that you believe in and practice, can reveal your individuality to an admissions committee.

List all the virtues that you think are important to living a happy, ethical, and successful life. Is trust an important thing to you? Write it on your list of virtues next to any of the others that you feel are really crucial to strong character. The following list of virtues can help you get started in your choices. The thing to remember here is that you need to limit your final choices to three virtues after you've compiled your list.

Faith/fidelity	Trust
Hope	Justice
Honesty	Perseverance
Patience	Temperance
Courage	Loyalty
Compassion	Humility

After you've made a list of your choices, look up the definitions of each virtue you've chosen. Then, write your own definition for each of those virtues, expanding on the dictionary definition. Once you've done this, review the list and choose three virtues that you can talk about at length. A good way to narrow them down is to choose the ones that you can identify easily in terms of how they have been present in your own life. Perhaps you are "dedicated" to something and the virtue of perseverance has helped you accomplish something special. You might have experienced the value of patience and have something to say about that virtue's influence in your life. Write anything that comes to mind about these qualities, including examples from your life and your definition of what the virtue really is. Then write why you think each one of your choices is important to your life. You might also consider writing the negative definitions and examples for each virtue you've chosen. Honesty is not about telling the truth because you're afraid of being caught in a lie, for example. If you can then explain what honesty really is, in your own words, you've revealed something unique about your perspective on life.

All your thoughts and reflections on important virtues give an admissions committee an insightful image of your values and character. Any essay that speaks to these issues is working in your favor.

4. Discuss Three Significant Lessons You Have Learned

MOST OF us who have gone to school know that we often learn more outside of class and away from homework than we ever do in our academic lives. Both the academic school and the School of Life are important in helping us grow into productive, happy individuals. It's what we do with what we learn in either atmosphere that determines our success in life.

As you approach college life, your ability to combine what you learn in and out of the classroom becomes more and more important. College admissions committees are looking for individuals who will bring more than a knowledge of books and lectures to their campuses. Truly successful students can bring real life to the lecture hall or the research paper and synthesize experience with academic information. Your learning experiences outside of the classroom can convey a tremendous amount of valuable information to the admissions team about the kind of "learning person" you are.

Some of the things that you have done or experienced have taught you special lessons that have become a part of your character. They are a force in the unique momentum that has

helped make you the gen-
uine individual that you
are today. No one else has
had experiences identical to
yours, nor has anyone else
left those experiences with
the insights or reflections
that you've kept with you.
Write any particular events
in your life that taught you
something you will always
remember and value. We're
not talking about your trip

> Your learning ex-
> periences outside
> of the classroom can
> convey a tremen-
> dous amount of
> valuable information
> to the admissions
> team about the kind
> of "learning person"
> you are.

to Paris here or the time you were working on the yearbook
staff. That's typical high school adventure and pretty flat subject
matter. Try to go outside of mundane experiences and think
about some event that changed you and taught you something.
List as many things as you can and then choose three of them as
the most important ones. Stuck? Can't think of anything? Here
are some questions that may help you with answers:

- Did you ever lose something that you thought was valuable and discover something better in its place?
- Have you ever had to react to circumstances in your life
  that opened your eyes to some hidden quality that you
  possess?
- Is there any job or activity that you *had* to do—but dis-
  liked doing—that ended up paying valuable dividends
  in the long run?
- Have your friends taught you anything about yourself?
- Is there anything that you didn't think you could accomplish or were afraid to try that you managed to complete?

Once you've put together the three experiences that taught
you lessons, you should write as much about each experience

as possible and explain *why* the event was a valuable learning experience. When you've finished writing your notes on each experience, move on to the fifth activity.

5. Tell Us About Three Memorable Experiences You Have Had

THIS SECTION may seem at first to be very similar to what we talked about in the previous section ("Lessons Learned"), and in some ways they may overlap. After all, experiences *can* teach us lessons about our lives. There's a difference here, though, however subtle. The emphasis here is on *description* of some significant experiences that you've had in your life, detailing what happened and how it affected you. Don't confuse the "memorable experience" with experiences that are impressive or exciting. The tendency for many people when they try to recall a memorable experience is to talk about a vacation excursion of some kind. Such an event, although it may be memorable for many reasons, is not so much a single experience as it is a collage of many experiences that were each unique and combined to create a treasured number of memories. In this exercise it's the little things that count, not just the big picture.

One student who responded to this section described a singular experience that she had on a vacation trip with her aunt to the Middle East. While walking in a market place in Istanbul, she and her aunt were approached by a man who offered to buy the student from her Aunt Gertie for a negotiable sum of money and goods. After the initial shock subsided, Aunt Gertie explained to the man that she couldn't sell her niece and quickly outlined the hidden defects of the student to the eager Turkish "entrepreneur." After hearing that the student couldn't cook, had a bad temperament, and was very expensive, the Turk politely dropped his offer and vanished into

EXAMPLES OF
MEMORABLE EXPERIENCES

Here are some examples of memorable experiences that may help you begin this section:

- An event that happened to you with one of your parents that helped you to get to know them in a more meaningful way.

- Something that you saw happen to someone or many other people that made you think about yourself or life itself in some new light.

- Something that you did that changed your life . . . and that you can't do again the same way. (A rite-of-passage experience such as a first date or your driving test is this kind of experience.)

- Any discovery that comes from what would have seemed to be a small event but that had a significant outcome.

- An experience that reveals the importance of deeds and not words in understanding the reality of human character. (It's one thing for someone to say he or she is your friend—quite another when you see it proven by action.)

the crowded market. Now, this kind of experience is certainly a unique one and is not a long story about the marvels of Turkey that we can all hear about in a travelogue. This story was used as the opening paragraph in a successful essay that discussed the value of life and experiences beyond the trip to Turkey. It was a great place to begin the essay.

So, memorable experiences aren't always the momentous ones. Some very striking experiences that stay in the memory may have lasted only seconds but still create strong impressions and thoughts that reveal the kind of person you are and display the depth of your character.

Think about yourself for a while before you get down to writing too much in this section. Recall your childhood, your adventures with friends and family, and all the "firsts" that have happened to you in what has been a very full life. Start writing these events and collect as many as you can in note form. Choose three with which you're comfortable and that you feel you can discuss in some meaningful way. Avoid anything that's not PG-13 for obvious reasons. Remember, you are trying to find experiences that say something unique and revealing about your character and person.

When you've chosen the three experiences, try to describe them with as much detail as possible. What were you seeing and feeling? What did things look like? Where were you and when did it happen? What did you hear in your head and outside of it? After you've pondered these questions, write about what you were thinking during the experience and afterward. One last question: Why do you remember this experience? When you're finished with this exercise, go on to activity 6.

6. Discuss a Failure That Taught You Something

A LONG time ago Bob Dylan wrote, "There's no success like failure, and failure's no success at all." Failure does have an element of success woven into it. What a person does with a failure or setback can turn what may seem a disaster into something very valuable. The movie comedy *Airplane* was rejected by dozens of Hollywood executives before it was finally picked up and became one of the top-grossing films of all time. (The script for the film went through more than twenty-five rewrites before it was sold!) There are hundreds of stories about people who failed miserably for years but whose persistence wouldn't allow them to deny their dreams. Eventually they became "overnight success stories." One thing we all have in common is failure. What we do with our failures sets us apart from one another.

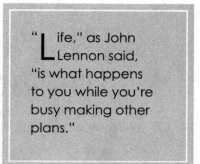

"Life," as John Lennon said, "is what happens to you while you're busy making other plans."

The "failure that taught me something" theme is a very popular one in many college essays because it allows the admissions committee to see how people handle adversity. It is a character indicator for the admissions team. They realize that college will not always be a smooth ride for students. "Life," as John Lennon said, "is what happens to you while you're busy making other plans." A student's life, like everyone else's, is fraught with interruptions of all kinds, even setbacks and disappointments. How you handle failure will determine your success in college and in life.

What kind of failures should you think about? That's a fairly personal question—even though there are some common setbacks that every high school junior or senior has had to overcome. Thousands of students have blown a course during the early part of a semester and then risen above their early difficulties to get the grade or master the subject. This is admirable in every respect, except that it doesn't really display your character in any unique way. Having your heart broken by your high school love and then growing to realize that the loss can be overcome, although important to your personal growth, is all too common and won't really demonstrate your strength of character to an admissions team. Some general topics in this area that have worked well in the essay are these:

TOPICS FOR THE "FAILURE THAT TAUGHT ME SOMETHING" THEME

- Learning to master a failure to communicate with an employer, parent, or some other significant person.

- Coping with the loss of a long-sought-after dream that came to nothing because of some fear to act or lack of readiness on your part.

- Understanding that being in the chorus or crew of the school play, when you wanted to have the lead role, taught you something about yourself and theater, as well. (This also occurs with students who didn't make the team in some sport and, instead of giving up the involvement in athletics in school, worked for the team in some other capacity, sharing in the experience of sport from another, equally rewarding, perspective.)

The important aspect of any question that deals with failure is the ability of the writer to turn the failure into a growth and learning experience. Avoid complaints or excuses in a subject of this type and concentrate on the positive side of a disappointing experience.

7. Respond to Three Quotes That Mean Something to You

ONE VERY popular and all-too-common technique that students use in the college essay or personal statement is to begin the essay with a quote from a famous person and use that quote as the keynote for their essay. Although this is not an unacceptable format for the essay, it *is* an often-used strategy; no one on the admissions committee is going to believe that you read German philosopher Friedrich Nietzsche just because you quote him in your essay. The ideas that flow from you *after* you've used the quote are the crucial part of an essay of this type.

The reason that I include this section on quotations and their use is not just to warn you that the use of quotations can be typical. Finding a strong quotation is not enough. Your *response* to a quote can open up a very special side of your intellect and character. It can move you in a direction that will become an integral part of your essay. You may never use the quote in your text, but the ideas it inspires may find their way into your essay.

Choose some quotes that mean something to you and that move you to think about the thoughts behind the quote and what they suggest to you. *Don't choose a quote and then explain it.* This isn't a test or an English composition. The quotes you choose should trigger a response in you that makes you want to write about an idea that holds great significance for you. You may have some favorite quotes from songs, poems, or writings by a favorite author. Perhaps a parent or a friend may have said something to you that started you thinking about the meaning of their words. The reasons why that quote is memorable may be just the catalyst you need to write something that you may wish to use in your essay.

Ideas can come from many sources. The inspiration that the words of others can give us is certainly fair game for a writer who wants to express a special part of his or her character in the college essay. The essential

> **Y**our *response* to a quote can open up a very special side of your intellect and character.

point here is that the quote should inspire you to express yourself about the importance of the ideas—not the quote itself—

and their significance to you. Respond to the quote in your notes—don't analyze it.

One final note on quotes. There are many books available filled with quotes that have been pulled from great literature, obscure poetry and speeches, and witty sayings and humorous lines from the history of the world's recorded wisdom. They can be a great source of inspiration, and they warrant a close look as you begin to prepare for your essay. (The bibliography of this book recommends some of those sources for quotes.) I suggest that you confine your choices to three major ideas and not dozens. If you find this too limiting, then collect as many quotes as you like *if* they help to open up your thought process and inspire you to write about ideas that express *you.* Consider the following as you do this exercise:

1. Choose quotes that inspire you and give you something to discuss that comes easily to you.

2. Don't think about using every quote that you find as a part of your essay. The ideas that each quotation generates are enough.

3. Don't explain the quotes. Let them create a thought response that you put on the paper in writing.

4. Relate the quote to *your* life and *your* vision.

5. Don't fill your essay with quotes. If you do decide to use one in your college essay, remember to attribute the source of the quote, and try to choose one that is brief. Extended quotes take up space in an essay that should be devoted in large part to your words and not those of someone else.

8. Remember Your Greatest Success

THE INITIAL reaction that most of my students have to this section of the profile is, "I haven't really had any great success yet." They couldn't be more mistaken. There is a saying in the Ten Commandments of Show Business that states, "Fame is what others give you. Success is what you give yourself." Many students mistake fame for success. So, what does success really mean? Success is a personal matter—different for each of us.

Remember that your greatest success should come from within you, not from the approval of someone else.

The best way to find out what *success* is for *you* may be to try to define it in your own words; consider the meaning of the word in the dictionary and see how it fits into your definition. The dictionary defines *success* as the "favorable termination of a venture," but there is much more to success for each of us than this. The way to fill your profile in this section is to think about what success is for you and commit the thoughts to paper. Consider all the examples of success in your life, no matter how small or secret. Think about what success is *not* and then write down those thoughts or illustrations. Very often in life we find out that what we thought was the prize at the end of an activity or undertaking was not the greatest benefit of the adventure. The success we achieve in anything can be very personal and without any public acclaim or recognition. These successes build crucial facets of our character. They can appear in many forms.

When you learn that the pot at the rainbow's end is filled with something better than gold, then you have a success story to tell. It may relate to the discovery of an unexpected value in a job or task you had to do or something that you learned about yourself that came unexpectedly while you were looking for something quite different. Remember that your greatest success should come from within you, not from the approval of someone else.

To make this part of the personal profile helpful to you, it's important that you write down everything that comes to you about success. Definitions, ideas, memories, negative definitions, examples from your life . . . anything that equals success for *you.*

9. Name Five Things That You Know

"KNOWLEDGE IS power." What you do with what you know can be an advantage in your life. What you do with what you know can also open countless doors that lead to wondrous experiences. One of the reasons education is so valuable is that it unlocks these doors to the unknown and allows you to explore new areas with a certain amount of wisdom and understanding. Formal education, however, is not the only way to learn about life.

You learn from your mistakes, successes, and the examples of others. The fact that everyone has something to learn from others suggests that everyone has something to teach others that has been learned from experience. In this section of the profile the goal is to write down all the things you can think of that you've learned from your experience and from your perception of life. There are many things that you know, and these bits of personal wisdom are part of who you are. They illuminate your ability to learn from living, and these discoveries, ultimately, are the most important kinds of knowledge. The things you know can also be unique and interesting, far beyond the facts that you've picked up in school courses. They will present a picture of the special you.

> There are many things that you know, and these bits of personal wisdom are part of who you are.

It's always exciting to see what students in the College Essay Workshops come up with when they tackle this section of the course. Some of the treasures that students have used in their essays that came from "things I know" are remarkably strong illustrations of their intelligence, character, and personality. A few examples of what college applicants have written down in this part of the profile, some of which ended up in their essays, are as follows:

- There is a time to give friendly advice and a time not to, because there are experiences everyone must go through without the bias of companions.
- People must know when they are the boss and when they are the employee; to confuse these roles is disaster.
- Love of the heart is more important than love of the face.
- When preparing a sauté, use oil with the butter so that the butter will not burn.
- Before you start to play a game, make sure you know the rules.

A solid way to approach the "things I know" problem is to make a list of everyday life experiences and then think about what you've learned by doing them. Activities such as shopping, working, playing, even driving are good places to start. These sample activities will suggest other areas of daily life to add as headings for lists of the things you've learned that have become useful to you in life. You really *know* a lot more than you realize, and this section of the profile can give you some information that will help to make your essay more personal and unique.

10. Discuss Your Definition of Happiness

THE CONCEPT of happiness is a tricky one. Even philosophers have grappled with what true happiness really is. One thing is

> Determining what makes you happy is a good way to start setting your goals and finding out what you really want from life.

certain: Everyone strives for happiness in his or her life. The Constitution of the United States maintains, for example, that "the pursuit of happiness" is one of our most fundamental rights. It would seem to follow logically that most people should have some idea of what they think happiness means to them. In most cases, however, people don't really think about their particular perspective of happiness very much. Give this some thought. When was the last time you sat down and wrote a list of the things that bring you happiness? Try to get a picture of what happiness really is to *you* in general terms.

Determining what makes you happy is a good way to start setting your goals and finding out what you really want from life. If you're going to write an essay for the admissions committee that gives an idea of what you're like as a human being, doesn't it make sense to know what makes you happy before you start to write your statement? Even if you don't use any of the ideas that come up in this section, you will have a fresh perspective on yourself, and you probably *won't* write about many things that really do not matter to you.

Make a list of all the things that make you happy. Think about ideas or experiences that give you happiness—things, objects, moments, sights and sounds, people and places, everything sensory that fills you with any kind of refreshing joy. I hope your list is a long one, but if it's hard for you to start because you're thinking of big ideas, then reverse yourself and begin with the little joys, because they count for a great part of your personal happiness. Ice cream, camping, days at the beach, good jokes, fine poetry, a solid line drive to left field, winning at chess, helping your little sister learn to skate . . . *anything qualifies that spells happiness for you.* After you've compiled this list, you're ready for the next step.

Once you've put together a random list of things that make you happy, go down the list and write *why* these items in your life make you joyful and give you such a lift. Think about what they *mean* to *you.* What special qualities do they bring to your life? The items on the happiness list may indicate a direction that your essay can follow or a topic that you might discuss in a paragraph later on in the process. Don't be reluctant. Write what comes to mind and then leave room at the bottom of the page in case you think of anything later that should be included in this section.

11. What Do Your Parents Remember About You?

ONE OF the great satisfactions from any kind of writing is the surprise of discovery that can come from research. You're doing some background work right now on one of the most important topics you'll ever cover: you. Keep in mind that the audience is a serious one, too. The admissions committee expects you to know something about yourself beyond the facts on your brag sheet. They expect you to have some sense of yourself, a command of your own "history." Well, a good researcher always goes to the source to capture the information. Secondhand information is just not good enough when the story is an important one. Like Woodward and Bernstein, who cracked the Watergate cover-up, you have to do some footwork to find out where everything in the story began, who was involved, and what happened in the early stages of the story that may illuminate the facts you already have. What better place for you to go than to one or both of your parents? After all, they were there at the beginning.

What better place for you to go than to one or both of your parents? After all, they were there at the beginning.

Parents often have an illuminating perspective on your early life and development. Of course, there are also things about you that they don't understand. That's not the point in this exercise. The goal is to discover some valuable insights on you, and your parents may have a few "angles" on your life that you might use in your essay. It's time to talk to them about it.

Set up a time to interview your parents about *you*. Be businesslike about it; tell them that you'd like to talk to them about your early childhood and that you want to discuss any reflections they may have about you, from the past to the present. Ask them to consider incidents they recall that may have had some significance in the picture and history of you. Give them a day or two to get ready before you sit down with a tape recorder and note pad. Allow yourself a day to prepare the questions that you'll be asking them. Make sure your questions are written on the note pad, and figure that the interview will last about half an hour to an hour. This is a research exercise that may yield some great insights and information for your essay. Have fun with this and enjoy the experience. Even if you learn nothing that you can use in your college essay, you and your parents may leave the interview with a better understanding about yourselves.

Good interview technique is often crucial for getting the best information. Here are some ground rules that you should consider before you start:

1.   Conduct the interview in a comfortable setting. Try to avoid the dinner table—too many distractions, and the food gets cold, too.

2. Don't make a big deal about the tape recorder. Use one if you can; turn it on and forget about it. Use a fresh tape, and make sure you're in "record" mode.

3. Have your questions written on paper in advance. Don't wing it. If your parents see that you're prepared, they'll take it seriously, too.

4. Don't ask Yes or No questions. Ask your parents questions about events and memories that call for them to tell the story in their own words. You want them to recount things that you don't remember or that are vague in your recollection but that they may be able to reveal for you from their personal perspective.

5. Take an occasional note if they say something that needs follow-up but don't interrupt while they are talking. Let them give you their full, nonstop recall; then cross-examine them with the questions from your notes.

6. When the interview runs out of gas, end it with sincere gratitude and then go somewhere and write down some reflections on what you thought was memorable, without listening to the tape.

7. The day after the interview, set the footage counter on the recorder at zero at the beginning of the tape. Listen to the tape; each time you hear something that you think may work in the essay, stop the tape and note the footage number on a piece of paper. After you've heard the tape all the way through, go back and transcribe the usable material, using the footage numbers as reference points.

If you get anything that helps you with your essay preparation, you will probably know it immediately, but don't toss the tape if your family gives you what you think is a "flat" interview. There may be something on the tape, no matter how seemingly insignificant, that you may use later on as you're writing. Log the information that you think is interesting, revealing, or hilarious. Any facts that tell about you from a new

INTERVIEW QUESTIONS

1. Tell me anything that you can recall about the day I was born.

2. Is there anything that you can remember about me as an infant or child that was particularly unique or interesting to you? Any memorable moments or impressions?

3. What was I like as a baby?

4. What were my first words?

5. What did you learn about being a parent from raising me as a child?

6. Is there anything I do or say now as an adolescent that I did or said as an infant or child?

7. How have I changed most, other than my size?

8. What are the first words that come to mind that best describe me in your eyes?

9. What have I learned best since being a baby, in your estimation?

10. Who am I named after and why?

angle can become valuable, so write down whatever moves or impresses you as you listen to the tape *alone*. (It's *your* story, so don't write down your information with anyone prompting you. You'll know what works.)

Questions? The most common query that I've encountered from my students in the College Essay Workshop is "What questions should I ask?" For a sample list, please refer to the interview questions above.

Of course, there are many questions that you may devise on your own, but if you're stuck, these will give you some information that may yield good material for your profile. Have fun with this exercise and remember that even a small bit of positive information may tell something unique about you, your character, and your sense of self.

12. What Are Your Earliest Memories?

INTERVIEWING YOUR parents will reveal things about yourself that you may not have known, but it may also do something else. It may jog your memory about your early childhood and open up hidden recollections that had been sleeping for fifteen years. Everyone has early memories of childhood that stand out for one reason or another. Write down the memories that you have, regardless of how insignificant they may seem. *Anything* that has to do with you may be of use in one way or another when you reach the writing phase of the essay. Write it all in detail on the sheet for this section.

13. What Is an Education Supposed to Provide?

THE REASON that you're going through this nerve-jangling college application process is to be accepted at the college of your choice, right? The entire ordeal of putting everything together in the application, sweating out the SATs, and writing this essay or personal statement is aimed at achieving the goal of college acceptance at an institution that you respect. You're hoping to spend the next four years of your life there, and that is a very significant chunk of your time. Why are you going through all this? What do you expect to get from the college experience? These sound like fairly easy questions, don't they?

Many students who face these questions tell me that they expect to be trained for a career. They know that a university education is a prerequisite to success in any professional field. Admissions committee members understand that this is one motivation that students have for attending an institution of higher learning. But they also expect their applicants to have other motives for going to college. The faculty, staff, and admissions officers at the college of your choice do not consider themselves part of a job-training program for students. They're looking for people with motives that are more profound than making some good connections, grabbing a diploma, and earning a good salary after graduation. What are the values that you place on a college education, beyond the fact that you need a B.A. to get a good job? You may not be called on to explain these values explicitly in your college essay, but the *spirit* and *worth* of the goal that you seek should be part of the energy that drives you to write your essay. You need to know in your own words, written clearly on a sheet of paper, what a college education is supposed to provide you.

> They're looking for people with motives that are more profound than making some good connections, grabbing a diploma, and earning a good salary after graduation.

Would you buy a car and drive it away without any idea of why you made the purchase? Whenever you look at a menu in a restaurant before eating, you choose your entrée and dessert for various reasons, not just because you *have* to eat or simply because the food has the right combination of carbohydrates and protein to keep you alive. Knowing why you are going to college is also much more involved than doing it because it's expected of you. You need to know the answer to this question, not only because you may wish to mention it in a paragraph of your essay but also because your experience in college will be enhanced if you know why you are there.

Think about all the reasons that a college education is important to you as an individual. Classes, activities, and people—consider *everything* that college is and then ask yourself *why* it is valuable to you. Write these thoughts as clearly as you can. Your reasons for going to college can reveal a very significant aspect of your character, and we already know how admissions committees feel about the character strength of their applicants. Write your responses to this section and then move to the next activity.

14. List and Describe Five Special Things About You

PEOPLE DIFFER from each other in hundreds of ways. Physically, no two human beings have identical fingerprints, tones of voice, or brain waves. People are all one-of-a-kind creatures. You are the only person in history who is sitting or standing where you are right now and reading these words at just this moment. You are special—a one-time-only individual.

A difficult dilemma that many people face in high school is the pressure to conform—socially, creatively, academically, in every way. It is a time when young people are searching for and defining their self-image and public image. It is usually a pretty tough time because everything is changing so quickly and the world seems full of new ideas, new people, new freedoms, and new responsibilities. In the face of all of these challenges, many people seek shelter from the chaos in the anonymity of the crowd.

Some adolescents respond to their high school years by attempting to mold their lives to a standard of behavior that avoids anything that is unique or special, beyond displaying special abilities in academics or athletic pursuits. It may seem okay to be a star student or athlete—that kind of "special" is accepted by most standards in college-preparatory high schools. Although these kinds of special qualities are laudable and important, they certainly are not the only qualities that set individuals apart from others in a unique way.

What makes you different from everyone else? Write anything that comes to mind here. Are you very tall or very short? Does your red hair make you unique? Are you extremely good with children or elderly people? Do you have a knack for working on cars or electronic instruments? Do you take terrific photographs? When I was a graduate student at Berkeley, I knew a fellow student whom stray dogs followed everywhere. It was a nuisance, at times, but it certainly was special.

Any special ability, quality, or skill that you have beyond the academic or athletic can help you fill out your profile and may very possibly be used in your essay in a number of ways. Take a good look at yourself. Ask yourself what it is about you that is a little different or special in any area of endeavor. Ask your friends to tell you anything they notice that's both unique and printable. Record these things and any reflections you have about these qualities. Categories that may help you can be as general as these:

- Physical uniqueness
- Interests or tastes
- Beliefs (not religious, but personal beliefs)
- Talents
- Habits
- Idiosyncrasies
- Recurring situations

Don't get caught in the mistaken belief that you aren't unique unless you have star status in something that everyone applauds. You are special in many ways, as everyone is. Write down those unique details about yourself and then say a few words about *why* these things about you are special.

15. What Is Your "One-Sentence Philosophy of Life"?

BY NOW, if you've been writing thoughts and ideas for each of the profile sections, your sense of what you believe and think about your life should be more clear. You have been immersed in the untapped reservoir of personal data that describe *you;* you discovered information about yourself from which a unique person has emerged, complete with ideals, a history, and perspectives that combine to make you see how you are a special person. This immersion, or diving deep into who you are, may have given you occasion to think about a big topic: *life.*

All of us sooner or later arrive at certain conclusions about life. Our experiences and responses to life eventually cause us to form a kind of philosophy that may explain why life behaves the way it does and how to negotiate the events of the future. A philosophy may be a definition of life, an explanation of existence, or a rule that seems to apply to everyday living. Most of us have several philosophical angles on living. These personal views may include spiritual philosophies, political philosophies, and economic and artistic philosophies that correspond to both the everyday part of life and the "big picture," as well.

> Ask yourself what it is about you that is a little different or special in any area of endeavor.

> If you had to explain life to an alien from another galaxy, what would you say to the individual in simple terms?

You have various philosophies of life and may never have written them down. Write them now in your own words. Think about life in any terms you wish, from everyday living to life as a concept or idea. What is life to you? What does life have to offer? If you had to explain life to an alien from another galaxy, what would you say to the individual in simple terms? Perhaps this will be an opportunity for the poet in you to emerge. Let your philosophy voice itself in poetic metaphor or simile. Write down each philosophy and then discuss each one individually in your own words. Explain in a brief paragraph *why* you believe each philosophical statement to be true, with one paragraph for each belief. If you think "Life is like a bowl of Jell-O," you have to be ready to write about why you see the world as a wiggling, semiliquid, semisolid, transparent, translucent mass of lecithin and sugar. Good luck!

16. What Is the Funniest Thing That Ever Happened to You?

VETERAN COMEDIANS know that, in comedy, timing is everything. *Funny* is an elusive concept. What may seem hilarious to one person may not be so to someone else. Any attempt at telling a funny story carries with it a risk. There is a technique to successful comedy, as well. Comics know the importance of timing and delivery, never giving away the punch line until the right moment.

You may have a story in your life that says a tremendous amount about you and your sense of humor. If you have the gift of humor and the ability to tell the story well, then this section of the profile may help your essay. Admissions officers love funny stories that convey a sense of the student as a person. These stories break the boredom for admissions people, and a funny story can be very effective. However, it can also be disastrous if the story is not funny, is in bad taste, or is just plain stupid.

Write down any laughable tales about yourself and then try them out on your friends, family, and even some people on your high school faculty who don't know you very well. You may get laughs galore, and if so, you may be able to use the story in your essay, but the risk is yours. The anecdote has to be more than funny, you see. It also has to tell us something about you as a person—something positive and illuminating about your insight, sense of self, and writing ability. Let your trial audience *read* your story. Don't read it for them. You won't be there to jazz up your delivery for the admissions committee when they get your essay. The words will have to elicit laughter from the page.

Don't feel bad if you don't have a funny story about yourself. College admissions teams don't require you to tell a joke in your essay because entertainment is not the point here. Remember, you can't be all things to all people. Be yourself, and you're a long way toward writing a good essay, laughs or no laughs.

17. What Makes the World Go Round?

ONE WORD most often used to describe any great leader is *visionary.* History and experience tell us that leadership demands a sense of vision, an ability to understand the significance of present-day events and their impact on the future. Individuals with a sense of vision aren't necessarily prophets or fortune-tellers, but they are certainly students of their world. Having a sense of vision isn't as mystical as it may sound. Vision is a combination of many things that, when synthesized, allow a person to make intelligent choices and avoid costly disasters.

Awareness, respect for history's lessons, and decisive action are the essentials of a good sense of vision. They are also the cornerstones of a successful college career, and they can be demonstrated in a college application essay in many ways.

Obviously, you are already exercising your "sense of vision" in several aspects of your life. You may have made decisions about a career choice—definitely something that requires you to think on a visionary plane. Taking stock of your talents and dreams and making decisions about what you would like to do in the world is no easy matter, but everyone has to put reality and dreams together in order to reach goals. What does this have to do with the college application essay? Plenty.

If you take a look at what you see happening in the world around you, there is good chance that you'll come to some conclusions about human behavior and that you'll have some questions about it, too. You may have some strong feelings about why the world is the way it is today, based on what you've learned and observed both in and out of the classroom. Write them—both the phenomena and the reasons for why you think certain conditions exist.

> You have a world-view already, and it's part of who you are, even though you may not have expressed it in written terms until now.

You're not being asked to solve the world's problems here, but you should have some thoughts in your prewriting profile about what you see and feel about the planet you've inherited. You can't have a sense of vision if you don't think about what's going on around you and why it's happening the way it is. Just writing it down on a sheet of paper can begin to give you a concrete idea of what your worldview is. You have a worldview already, and it's part of who you are, even though you may not have expressed it in written terms until now. Think about some of the things that concern you about your world, politically, culturally, economically, and socially. Write down your thoughts about each area of concern. Here's a partial list of things you might think about:

- The environment
- World hunger
- Art and music
- War and political security
- Money
- Poverty and wealth
- Space travel and exploration
- Aging
- Medicine
- Technology

Take any topic of significance to you and write something about what you *think* and *why*. What do you see? What's your vision? If you see great things coming, needs that must be fulfilled, or problems that must be solved in any area, write them and talk about them in your own words. Remember, you're putting together a viewpoint, *not a list of solutions*. You may have some very clear suggestions for improvements and they may be very valid ideas, but approach this less as a blueprint for saving the world than as a statement of your vision.

Is the automobile more than a means of transportation? Will water one day be more valuable by the ounce than gold? When sports heroes and movie stars become our prominent figures in society, what does that say about the direction in which humanity is moving? You live in the world and see what is happening to it. The insights and opinions you have, supported by your observations, are your vision. What do you think? Record it.

18. Picture the Five Places You've Been That Impressed You the Most

THE AMERICAN writer Gertrude Stein once described a city in California with a single sentence: "There is no 'there' there." Although this impression of the place reflects Ms. Stein's opinion and probably meets with some disagreement on the part of that town's current residents, it does illustrate something that you can use in completing this section of the profile. Our perceptions of the places that we visit and our memories of different places in which we have lived can say a great deal about our insights and abilities to observe phenomena. Again, it is the awareness of detail that is most important here. All of us have been to places that had an impact on us in some way, either favorably or otherwise. What are some of the places you remember in this way?

The reasons "why" we came away from a particular town, street, garden, or house with lasting impressions are fundamental illustrations of our insights into experience. We're not talking about the "oohs" and "aahs" of a vacation to Hawaii, however. The details and reasons why a place is fixed in your memory are important in this exercise. If you are impressed by a place because of its beauty, what *exactly* are the beautiful *details* that made your experience of it so memorable? If a trip through a poverty-stricken neighborhood in a South American city moved you to reflect and has stayed in your memory bank, what *details* struck you and *why* was the moment so meaningful? This is the

> If you are impressed by a place because of its beauty, what *exactly* are the beautiful *details* that made your experience of it so memorable?

type of response that requires your sensitivity to sensory detail, both personal and objective. If you're going to describe a vacation experience in your essay, you will be much more effective if you focus on a striking experience, something that is meaningful beyond the joy of just being there.

Too often a student will use a vacation as a topic of the college application essay and proceed through a litany of cities, countries, and famous spectacles that are at best nothing more than a travelogue. This kind of approach is a waste of time and doesn't give the admissions committee any idea of what you *think* or the keenness of your perceptions. Reflections such as, "My trip to Europe taught me that although all of us have different cultures, we still share many things in common," though true in essence, is also typical and is a common, often-heard sentiment. Your impressions in a case such as this should demonstrate *how* people are different as exemplified in your own experience and in what particular instances you witnessed the essential similarities that cross all borders and oceans.

Anyone who can afford the airfare can travel. That doesn't mean they've had momentous experiences in Europe or Asia just because they made the trip. Even seeing historic buildings and visiting famous monuments is little more than being "live" in a postcard setting. What a place can teach us about ourselves and our fellow humans is much more important to our character growth than a ride down the Seine on a *bateau-mouche*, however romantic it may have been. Don't let the "romance" of the trip or the spectacle of a scene obscure the important details and personal impressions that you may have. What you feel and think about a place are equally crucial to illustrating your sensitive nature in the essay.

How do you capture the importance of the places that impressed you? Jot down specific events and your feelings, thoughts, and memories of actual experiences. Try for exact detail and describe the moment as well as overall impressions. Your encounter with one person on a train to Berlin will be far more revealing of your sensitivity to a place than a general description of all West German train travelers. Often your memories of a particular street in Rome, detailed and alive, will give your essay more impact than a review of a trip across Italy that tries to say *everything*.

19. What Is Your Favorite Social Activity?

WHAT DO you like to do with other people? Why do you like this activity and what do you derive from the doing of it? Any kind of social activity—dancing, athletics, traveling with friends, picnics, amusement park outings—can be used for this part of the profile. The point to emphasize is the *social aspect* of the activity—the people involved and not just the activity itself. In addition, you should try to explain *why* you enjoy this kind of experience. Emphasize the elements that make it valuable and something that you treasure doing. In the event that you have a few social activities that fit this bill, do the same for each one. Try to be as thoughtful as you can be about the reasons you enjoy your social experiences. Just saying you like to go to rock concerts "because it's fun" isn't enough. Remember, answering the question "why" is important, so tell us *why* any social experience is fun. The activity should reflect your insight and appreciation of the value of the experience.

20. What Is Your Favorite Intellectual or Artistic Activity?

WHAT DO you like to do that challenges your brains? Is there a creative outlet you practice that takes your mind and spirit to a special place? If you like to read, play chess, challenge your computer, write poetry, play a musical instrument, or design anything, tell us about it on paper and then discuss why you enjoy doing it. This is an exciting opportunity to describe the journey that you take in your mind as you practice the mental or artistic exercise that you love. There's a palpable joy, an exhilaration that we can embrace when our minds become involved in creative mental play. One of my students wrote a marvelous essay on his discovery of the study of dance, and the freedom and creative exuberance that captured a tough kid from a tough neighborhood with the grace and poise of motion to music. Another of my students told of the wonderful saga of building a robot at an MIT science camp, taking us through the creation of a nuts, bolts, and wired tight "little guy" that won the prize and changed the student's life and his choice of career. The focus on any activity in this realm is the description of process—a great vehicle for an epic journey of your mind in the world of mental and creative challenge. Whether your "thing" is building robots, blowing glass, creating websites or computer games, playing Chopin etudes, or reading the poetry of Rainer Maria Rilke, the heart of the matter is revealing the journey you take when you play in the world of your imagination.

21. Describe Yourself to a Stranger

WITHOUT ASSUMING that you have any more than the normal degree of human vanity, you probably look at yourself in the mirror every day. What do you look like when you see yourself? Be as objective as you can be, without sacrificing any creative comparisons that may come to mind. If you had to describe yourself to a stranger who had to pick you out of a large crowd, how would you describe yourself? Be as specific as you can be, and be thorough as well. Hair color and height aren't nearly enough because you're in a crowd of people and some-one actually has to find you. What are you wearing? How do you walk? What shape does your face have? Do you have any resemblance to someone we'd recognize? Try to have fun with this part of the profile. It might offer you an option if you're stuck for a place to start in your essay.

22. Tell the Story of a Fear You Conquered

FEAR IS a common human response to certain phenomena. It is a natural component of life for all living creatures. Perhaps in one of your classes in school you have discussed the idea of "flight or fight," the two most common behavioral reactions to fear. How you handle your fears—whether you choose to fight something that gives you cause to be afraid or decide to run for cover, electing to avoid the situation—can often indicate something very significant about your character.

Of course, there are many times when flight is a wise course of action; and on such occasions to fight an object of your fear can be perilously foolhardy. Everyone tries to avoid dangerous situations in life, such as deranged individuals, angry bears, and bad parts of town, and these instances of flight from danger are smart responses to the messages fear sends. The fears that paralyze you or hold you back from experiences that can be beneficial in some way are, on the other hand, well worth fighting. Any fear in your life that stands in the way of your growth as a person or one that inhibits your

> If you had to describe yourself to a stranger who had to pick you out of a large crowd, how would you describe yourself?

optimum performance in some important part of your life usually is conquerable if you work hard to face the problem, seek help from people who care about you, and learn the facts behind the unknown that often frightens you.

Sir Laurence Olivier, perhaps the greatest dramatic actor of the twentieth century, confessed in an interview conducted during the later part of his life that he had suffered from acute stage fright for ten years during the high point of his acting career. Night after night he would go out on the stage and never be able to remember the next line until the very moment he was to deliver the words. He begged his fellow actors please to refrain from looking him in the eye during one performance for fear that he would completely fall apart if they sensed his terror on stage! In spite of this problem, Olivier continued to act and managed finally to regain his confidence. He often thought of retiring during this period and even planned to make the announcement one evening as the Queen of England and the playwright Noel Coward sat in the audience of the Old Vic Theatre. Somehow he managed to hang on, and he overcame this potentially ruinous affliction.

> You might find that you have done something really remarkable in locking horns with an obstacle in your life and that your success merits mention in your college essay.

People, in every stage of life, have to face fears that can cripple their lives if they let them control their actions. In this section of the profile you should write down any fears that you've had to face and conquer on the way to becoming the person that you are. Portray your experience of fear and what it did to you; then discuss the course of action you undertook to overcome the problem. The conquering of any fear is a success story of significance. You might find that you have done something really remarkable in locking horns with an obstacle in your life and that your success merits mention in your college essay.

An important thing to keep in mind as you write about your mastering of a fear is that such an experience is a positive thing. Everyone has experienced fears they had to conquer in order to grow. Admissions officers can appreciate the importance of this kind of personal victory and how it contributes to your ability to handle adversity during your college life and beyond. Concentrate on the positive outcome of your experience and the things that you learned in the process of taking on the beast of fear and taming it.

One student's response to this part of the profile can serve as a strong example of its worth in the essay. He suffered from a fear of drowning from early childhood and as a result was terrified to enter water that reached his waist. He had been thrown into the ocean as a two-year-old child by an overzealous father who thought the experience would introduce the boy "naturally" to the wonders of the water. Because of this baptism that nearly drowned him, the boy was unable to swim throughout his early childhood, and the mere thought of going into the ocean or jumping into a pool at the deep end was a paralyzing trauma. After years of fear and the harassment of friends and siblings, the boy decided to teach himself to swim, with the aid of an understanding friend. He was fourteen years old at the time, and he and his buddy slipped into a private club pool at night after the club had closed. With perseverance, practice, and the help of his friend, the boy learned to relax in the water at any depth, and he learned to swim. Immediately a new world of experience opened up to him, and the confidence he gained from conquering this fear enabled him to answer many other challenges in his life. He titled the essay "Sink . . . or Swim."

23. Discuss Three Goals You Have in Life

IF A bicycle is not moving forward, it will fall down. That's what one goal motivator tells his students when discussing the importance of goals in life. Each of our lives is certainly meant to be in motion. Goals help us know in what direction we want to move. Goals can help define the character of an individual in many ways, because they illustrate what he or she wants and what he or she thinks is important. Setting goals requires choices and decisions . . . and hard work. Goals are more than dreams. They are challenges that we choose to meet and destinations that we strive to reach.

What goals have you set for yourself? There are several ways to approach writing down your goals, and this process itself is an important part of achieving them. Big goals are made of small goals. When you write your goals, you should think in terms of long-range, intermediate, and immediate goals. Long-range goals, such as "I want to be a doctor," take time and preparation. If you're going to talk about what you want to be in your essay, then it makes sense to have a plan that takes the goal out of the dream phase and into the action phase. This is why smaller, intermediate goals are so important.

In the college essay or personal statement, students often discuss their career goals in idealistic terms, outlining why they want to be a member of a particular profession and how they hope to help humankind with their work in the field they are choosing. These are admirable sentiments, but in the college essay they often come off as a "big dream" unless the statement has something more substantial than "I want" attached to it. Dreams do come true—but only with a plan and dedication to the work that will make them realities.

Do you have a dream? Then what is your plan? How have you prepared for it? Are you doing something about your dream right now? Why did you choose this goal? Why is this goal the right one for you? These are all questions that you have to answer if your goal is realistic. It doesn't matter how far-fetched the goal may seem to others if you have a plan and you are moving toward it. Maybe the reason you chose a particular college for your future is part of your long-term goal. Say so. Perhaps your summer jobs are goal-related. Write this fact in the profile section and explain that you made the choice to work in a hospital because you are planning on a medical career. There is a saying that "Chance favors the prepared person." It certainly is true that the credibility of your goal will be much greater in the eyes of admissions officers if they see that you are a person who not only has a dream, but knows the path to its achievement.

As the actor, John Wayne, said, "You can talk the talk, but can you walk the walk?" If you can illustrate the preparation you have undertaken and outlined to reach your goals, then you have a strong statement in your college essay. Courses you've taken in high school, summer jobs, extra study and reading, and the choice of an undergraduate college because of its particular strengths in your chosen field of endeavor show preparation for a long-term goal and will support your quest for acceptance into a college. These actions say, "I'm a person of action, a winner with a plan—someone who follows through on my dreams."

24. List Ten Things You Like and Ten Things You Don't Like at All

DON'T PONDER over this too long. React to your immediate feelings. What do you like? A particular ice-cream flavor, an actor or actress, a sport, a holiday, the way something is done? If you saw the film *Bull Durham,* you might recall the scene in which Kevin Costner tells Susan Sarandon what he likes. It's a list that covers a panorama of experience and it identifies his taste, strength of character, and imagination immediately. You can do the same thing here. This is a pure list, with no explanations necessary.

> Do you have a dream? Then what is your plan? How have you prepared for it?

Your likes and dislikes define a particular side of you that is unique and yet understandable. What do you dislike? Be specific. Dates that show up late? Cold hamburgers? Chewing gum on the sidewalk? Sitcoms with canned laughter? There are a million specific things in everyone's life that we choose to love and hate, like or dislike, and they need no explanation. If you later want to make your list longer than ten items, do so. If you choose to use this part of the profile as a segment of your essay, you should limit your mention of "likes and dislikes" to no more than ten or so each or you may overdo the approach. Quality, not quantity, is essential here. Share your list with your mentor, friends, and family. Ask them if your choices tell them anything about you. Write down their answers and think about them.

A reminder that should be obvious by now: Exercise good taste and intelligence in your choices and keep everything you mention PG-13.

25. What Do Your Friends Say That They Like Most About You?

PEOPLE ARE drawn to others for countless and often fascinating reasons. Our friends know things about us that we have never noticed, the good and not so good, and yet they still care about us. Your friends are a valuable resource in this part of the

QUESTIONS FOR FRIENDS

1. What characteristics do I have that you think are unique or outstanding?

2. Is there any particular situation in our friendship that you remember that illustrates why we are friends?

3. In your opinion what is my strongest point?

4. What is my greatest weakness?

5. Why are we friends?

6. What five words would you use to describe me to someone? (cool, calm, decisive, etc.)

personal profile. If you can, interview them using the same techniques that you used with your parents. Be prepared before the interview with specific questions, as you were with your mother and/or father. Include your brothers and sisters in this part of the profile, if you'd like. They know you from a unique perspective.

Sometimes it's not easy for people close to you to be serious when asked important questions such as, "What do I contribute to our friendship?" or "What exactly do you like about me as a person?" Perhaps the best way to deal with interviewing your friends is to go with whatever they say in response to your questions, at first, and then follow up with an attempt to get a straight comment from them about you. It is an interview, and if you demand too much control, it won't really yield honest information from your subjects. Allow whatever happens and get what you can on tape and in your notes. Even a single statement from a friend about you or your character can be a terrific way to begin a paragraph when you get ready to draft your essay. You're not looking for volumes in this part of the data resource—you're looking for ideas that you can use at just the right place later on in the process. If you are stuck for questions to ask your friends, please refer to the suggestions on page 68.

Answers to these questions should give your profile some interesting information. Thank your friends for their candor and contribution to your work and then listen to the tape later, by yourself, and transcribe exactly what they say on paper if it strikes you as revealing, interesting, or even funny. You'll know what's good when you hear it.

26. What Question Have You Always Wanted Answered and Why?

NOW I will ask you to pose a question of your own. The question should be something that has meaning for you and that asks for an answer that you truly care about and want to know. Our questions can reveal more about us than our answers do. What you want to know is a clear indication of what concerns you. Write down several questions that you'd like to have answered. After you've got the questions down on paper, go back and discuss *why* you want to know the answer or *why* the question is important to you.

Obviously, some of your questions won't have any answers, but you have to ask them nonetheless. Realize that your questions are a valuable part of your character and that you may spend a significant part of your life in search of answers to questions that affect us all. Scientists, artists, teachers, and any people who respond successfully to the questions life poses are a benefit to everyone. Something that you want to

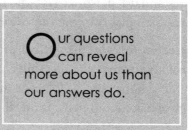

Our questions can reveal more about us than our answers do.

As soon as possible, begin writing a daily journal about what you see, think, and feel.

know and the reasons why it demands attention and serious inquiry may tell an admissions committee more about you than all your answers on the SAT. Think about it. The admissions officers will, too.

Now you have completed the 26-point profile, and you have something that can help you write a unique and informed college essay or personal statement. Go back over the profile responses that you gave and read them carefully. Note the sections that seem to be your favorites, the ones that say something about you that you feel is revealing or special. Underline ideas and statements that strike you as having a special quality. While you're reading this collection of information and ideas, you may discover additional thoughts that you'd like to include. *Write them down.* Once you've read everything over from beginning to end, take a break, then go on to the next chapter.

Strategy Notes

Begin Early. More and more students are preparing for their college application essays the summer before, or during, their junior year. Though specific essay questions for many colleges may not yet be available at that time, you can start developing a standard personal statement. This is a great time to begin practicing and trying out topic ideas.

Keep a Journal. As soon as possible, begin writing a daily journal about what you see, think, and feel. Be very detailed and specific about times, places, and sensory details, as well as impressions and perceptions that you may have about your daily activities. Not only is this good writing practice, but you may find that a topic evolves from some of your journal entries.

Use Your Summers. Plan the summer before your senior year wisely. Don't just hang out at the beach or in the neighborhood—do something challenging and noteworthy. Apply for an unusual job or get involved in something that will challenge your limits: Climb a mountain, become an intern for the summer, take a college course, participate in an organization that interests you. Take a "road less traveled" and keep a constant and detailed journal on the experience.

Be a Camera Head. This is a writing exercise that is meant to help you look at things in a different way. Spend some time every day describing an experience from a purely sensory level. (Fifteen minutes to a half hour will do the job.) Capture details that these observations or experiences record in your mind, but try to avoid any judgments or intangible concepts. Describe any experience or encounter—a meal; a trip by car; a walk; a place, person, or thing—and paint the images of the experience with concrete, vibrant detail. *Show* the experience and avoid telling about it. Use colors, shapes, action words, and similes. Make it live. Like a camera, get close-ups, pan around, tilt up and down, and dolly in and out. Focus tightly and get the scene on paper. Don't edit anything—just get the shots. Transfer this daily technique to your profiles and then to your essay drafts as soon as possible.

4

Go to Commercial

"There are three kinds of lies," Mark Twain once said. "Lies, damn lies, . . . , and statistics." The people who will read your transcripts and records will be aware that the SAT scores and other numbers that represent you may be misleading and not completely revealing of what you may have to offer their college community. They've seen "ace students" flunk out after one term in college. They know that there is more to being a successful college student than good grades. That's why they take care to read your essay. Like any consumer who reads the ingredients on a box before purchasing the product, the admissions officers want to get a good idea of what's inside you. In the college admissions process, you are "the product" and the admissions officers are "the market." How do you reach them?

Products are placed before the market through advertising. The word *advertise* is derived from a Latin term that means "to give valued attention to." The primary goal of all advertising

Like any consumer who reads the ingredients on a box before purchasing the product, the admissions officers want to get a good idea of what's inside you.

campaigns is to draw the attention of the consumer to the value of the product. If an ad can show the value of the product and create a lasting impression in the mind of the consumer, then the ad has done its job. This may be a very simple explanation of good advertising, but that's what an ad is supposed to do: show the product is valuable in a memorable way.

This year some 2.9 million students will apply to college. Not all of them will write a college essay, but most of them will have to write some kind of personal statement. They are your competition.

Take a walk in your supermarket and look at all the competing brands of soap, soup, soft drinks, and shampoo, and you will see the competition in the market. Most of these goods are basically the same as their competitors. If you look at the ingredients of two or three competing goods, it becomes evident that packaging is usually the thing that sets one brand apart from any other. Who has time to try every soap in America to find out which one is just right? An advertising agency tries to put a product in the best possible light and aims to do it in a way that will make the product stand out from its competition. The product is doomed if the ad just says, "Hey, look. This product has all the ingredients that all the other products have." Being like everybody else in the marketplace means death for the product. In order to make an impression on consumers, a product has to be different *as well as being at least as good as everything else* that's on the shelf.

At your age, you have probably seen more commercials than your parents have seen in their lifetimes. You have been the target of more advertising than any generation in the history of sales. You know what it's like to have something sold to you. If there was ever a group who should understand the value and techniques of advertising, then you are one of that group. This should help you as you write your college application essay because a large part of the process involves sales and marketing. There are dozens of students trying to win your seat in the freshman class of the college to which you are applying. The way you present your product to the admissions committee is the advertisement that will either differentiate you from the other products or make you appear to be just another applicant.

Because your college application essay is similar to an ad in many ways, you should be aware of some tried-and-true rules of advertising in order for your essay to be effective. These will serve as a guideline for what to write and how to write it and as a reminder about why you are writing. Every year some students write cute, "off-the-wall," imaginative essays. Most of these essays are great ads for the students who write them. But they are not the only way to reach the market of admissions committees. There are many ways to make an impression. The method used to put a product in its best light is determined by the product, not the approach of the ad. You are the product. What makes you unique is what will determine the approach you take in presenting yourself to the admissions officers.

Let's take a look at how the college application essay is similar to an advertisement. The college application essay must create a favorable image of you, just as a good ad must create a positive image of the product. That means that your essay should be positive and reveal qualities that are appealing to the audience that reads it. Highlight your strengths, values, and special qualities. Winning games and pulling A's aren't unique. Think about the positive discoveries you've made in your life and the values that you gained from experiences; make these unique examples a part of your essay. These are the favorable images that allow you to stand out from the crowd.

The two basic appeals that advertisements use to reach the market should also be part of your essay. The first is the factual approach, and the second is the emotional approach.

The factual approach in an ad usually describes the demonstrable characteristics of the product. It tells the consumer what the product is, how it works, and how it is made. Car commercials use this approach in part. The typical Mercedes ad always gives us a litany of the technical marvels and performance standards of the car. The key element in the factual approach is that there are *facts* to back up the boast that the product is a good one. In the college essay this means that if you tell the world that you are serious about something, you should be able to present some factual evidence. Statistics and performance are the foundation of the factual appeal to the admissions committee. A factual appeal alone, however, reads like a litany of proof and sounds boring and presumptuous. It always needs the emotional approach to support it.

The emotional appeal is an important part of your college application essay. The emotional approach appeals to the audience's need for or appreciation of love, security, prestige, respect, honor, or particular values and virtues that are important to that market. As you saw in chapter 2, the individuals who will read your essay are looking for certain values, qualities, feelings, and ideas that good candidates must exhibit to be able to succeed in college. If you neglect to consider these requirements when you write your essay, you lose an important advantage. For what do you stand? What do you believe? How do you feel about issues and why? What goes on inside of you that defines you? If you can answer these questions in your essay, then you have made an emotional

> The emotional appeal is an important part of your college application essay.

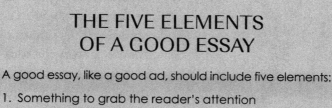

THE FIVE ELEMENTS OF A GOOD ESSAY

A good essay, like a good ad, should include five elements:

1. Something to grab the reader's attention
2. Simplicity
3. Realism
4. Sincerity
5. Surprise

appeal to the audience that means far more than reciting your grade-point average.

Both factual and emotional appeals should be reflected in your essay. They are fundamental to good communication. Facts and emotions need each other to be effective. Fact alone communicates only flat statistics or events. With emotional meaning behind the facts, there is a full picture of a person who knows the value of his or her life.

Getting Attention

THE BEST way to get attention is to do something different. This doesn't mean that you should be weird or outrageous. It means that you should accentuate a topic or idea that is not typical of everyone in the world. It means that the essay should focus on you and your life, which are unique materials. It also means that the opening sentence of your essay should be something direct and challenging. (The section on leads in chapter 6 can help you with this.) A strong attention-getting device in an essay can be a story that tells us about an important life

> **D**on't be afraid to write what you feel, as long as you have the courage to explain the worth of those feelings.

experience. It doesn't have to be funny or tragic to get attention. It is important to choose a story or idea that best illustrates who you are through a unique situation or condition in your life. Perhaps you had a blind friend in school who taught you how to see; or perhaps you learned about winning by losing. Your struggle to understand someone—a parent or peer—or your discovery of the beauty of a simple place that gave you an appreciation of nature and the importance of the environment—these are good subjects. Anything that has happened to you that taught you something or anything that reveals your sensitivity to the experience of your life is unique and special to you. These kinds of insights described in your essay will give you a special quality that is far from typical. At the same time, they will add emotional impact to your material. Don't be afraid to write what you feel, as long as you have the courage to explain the worth of those feelings. Great essays demand that you tell the whole truth. You must be yourself and place a value on your experience. The more "the real you" gets across in your essay, the more "different" you will be.

Simplicity

A CLUTTERED, overly complex, confusing essay can never achieve the goal of an effective advertisement. You can't tell the audience everything there is to know about you, so you have to narrow the story to important details and ideas. You must express yourself in easy-to-understand language. This means that you must use words that are conversational. Dragging out the thesaurus and using archaic words that appear in the SAT vocabulary test won't score you points in the application essay. These words sound contrived and unnatural and signal the reader that you're trying to be someone you're not. It's much better to write the essay in your own words. This will make your essay easier to read and give you a genuine, relaxed image. Every good ad is created with the knowledge that people trust and relate to honest, plain talk.

The law of simplicity also applies to the volume of information that your essay seeks to transmit. If your essay overloads the reader with fact, situations, or too many subjects, it dilutes your point and weakens your image. Concentrate on no more than five key ideas and develop them with solid detail and examples. Impact is your intention. If you overwhelm the admissions committee with too many ideas and facts, they will miss your statement's intended impact. Limit your essay to five solid lead-in sentences. If the admissions officers had time to read only the first sentence of each paragraph in your essay, would those sentences catch their attention?

Get Real!

COCA-COLA uses the classic lead line "It's the Real Thing" because the market always wants a product to be just what it claims to be. Realism, like simplicity, speaks the truth. We trust something that sounds real. Your college application essay must reveal who you really are to the admissions committee, and that means you must communicate real feelings, real events, honest thoughts, and actual moments in your life that tell about the real you. Trying to be or sound like someone you're not will never work. The admissions people are professionals. They've read hundreds of essays. They know the "real thing" when they see it. Give it to them and they'll believe you.

But give them hype and fabricated style or language, and they will see right through you.

Using realism in your essay means that you should concentrate on sounding like a real human being. Don't romanticize an event and try to turn your ideas into poetry and flowery sentiment. Hard facts and feelings always have an impact on a reader. The film *Platoon* is a success because it reveals the real feelings of young men in the Vietnam War. It doesn't attempt to sell us a "gung ho" line of propaganda about the conflict. In the same way, good advertisements attempt to place their product in a scene that is real and in an atmosphere that creates belief and trust. In the college application essay, you must tell the truth about yourself. The more your essay rings true, the more likely you are to have an impact. You want people to believe you. Are you real?

Some guidelines for achieving realism in your essay should be considered as you write. They are best described as questions you should ask yourself about your material:

- Do my words sound like me?
- Are my feelings and thoughts expressed in the essay, or am I just stating facts and ideas?
- When I describe something, such as an event, a condition, or an attitude, do I communicate on a sensory level or am I just telling the audience about what happened?
- Am I telling the truth?

Straight to the Heart

TOTAL IMPACT in advertising copy also depends upon the degree of sincerity that is communicated. You can't fake it. Sincerity is similar to realism, of course, because something that is sincere is true to life and, subsequently, more real. Sincerity in your college application essay is crucial. It demands that your words be honest and genuine. Your tone of voice will send the message of sincerity in the essay, and that means you have to sound like who you really are. The best way to ensure that your essay sounds like you is to read the final draft into a tape recorder and then listen to it with a mentor or an honest friend and decide if the words and sentences sound like you. If you were writing a letter to someone about whom you cared a great deal, you would pay close attention to the tone of the language. The way you would say things to the person in that letter would be important because you would want your sincerity to shine through the words. Your college application essay is no different. To achieve credibility, your tone should be clear, honest, and truthful.

Surprise!

THE FINAL element of impact in an advertisement is the use of surprise. The element of surprise is always effective in getting attention. Using surprise doesn't mean that you have to be shocking, however. In your college application essay the best way to use the element of surprise is in the leads that begin your paragraphs. Don't just open with flat, standard sentences. Occasionally give the reader something to chase. Hit the audience with a fact that surprises them and makes them want to know more. Ask a provocative question at the beginning of a paragraph, or use a quote that has a surprising impact. Once you have the readers' attention, you can take them "simply," "realistically," and "sincerely" through the development of your topic.

The topic of your college application can also use the element of surprise. How do you arrive at a "surprise topic" that allows you to

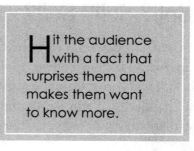

Hit the audience with a fact that surprises them and makes them want to know more.

reveal yourself honestly? Your personal profile from chapter 3 will give you information from which you can draw. Look at yourself, and find something that works as a metaphor in your life. Then use it as a device to reveal your values and your ability to express your understanding of experience. One student in the College Essay Workshop used the topic of nearsightedness and wrote about what she discovered about the world from wearing eyeglasses. Her essay revealed her sensitivity to the life around her. Another student used bicycle racing as a metaphor for conquering the "hills" of life. The topics that carry the impact of surprise are innumerable. One student chose her hands as a topic and discussed how they had figured greatly in her high school career. Another student used "the sounds that linger in the memory" as a surprise topic; other students have used the element of surprise with topics as diverse as shoes (they take you places), houses lived in (the secrets they hold), and pets (the things they know). Each of these surprise topics evolved from individual experiences.

The good college essays focus on little things that mean something special. Most college application essays lose the element of surprise by trying to sound intellectual or by listing endless achievements. These approaches are predictable and common. To their readers they are boring, and they reveal the fact that a boring person wrote them. For that surprise topic, look for the little moments and "taken-for-granted" instances in your life that say something special about you.

Sell? Sell? Sell?

NOTHING COULD be worse for any product than the hard-sell approach. If your college application essay seems like a hard sell, it will accumulate the negative associations that come with all hard sells. If you ignore the elements of impact mentioned earlier and try to sell your image to the admissions committee, you will lose your credibility. You'll seem like an immature kid who thinks that the admissions people will fall for your material. You'll lose them in the same way that bad ads lose the market. Stick with the traditions of advertising that work: honest, real, simple, and surprising. Don't plead your case. State it with feeling and truth. Don't brag

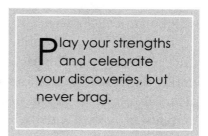

Play your strengths and celebrate your discoveries, but never brag.

about your stats. Prove that you have a human perspective. Don't criticize your competition. Accentuate your positive points and ignore the negative. Respect yourself and stand behind your values. Play your strengths and celebrate your discoveries, but never brag. Avis Rent-a-Car has made a mark in the business by selling the fact that they "Try Harder." They don't claim that they try the hardest.

Think TV

THE TELEVISION advertising "spot" can be a metaphor for your approach to the college application essay. TV spots are visual. Your essay should have a strong visual quality. Give your audience pictures that say who and what you are. For every concept or idea you generate in your essay, provide a picture, an illustration of that idea. It's the old "show and tell" routine. If you say or think that the environment of the planet is a crucial issue for you, then show why and how this is true for you. If you learned something special from your dad, show the reader with an illustration from real life that you really experienced. Talk is not enough. Show the reader how you came to feel the way you do.

Good TV ads are clean. They avoid excess language that is difficult for the audience to digest. They show us the product, tell us about the feelings the product elicits, and avoid clutter and confusion. The language is straightforward and simple. "Here it is. Here's how it works. Here's how it feels." No mumbo jumbo. No magic.

Effective TV ads place the product on center stage. They don't concentrate on the past, the competition, or topics that are unrelated to the product. Your college application essay should always be about *you,* first and foremost. It should never concentrate on what influenced you or your heroes more than it does on you. Everything that appears in your essay should keep exposing *you* as the primary focus of attention.

The market will never buy a product that it sees on TV if the ad fails to make them feel good. Good TV spots are positive. They accentuate the good of the product and never plead for understanding or compassion from the audience. Lighting, the angle of every shot, music, and tone of voice are always strong and confident. Your essay should be strong and confident, too. Place yourself in a spotlight. Choose angles that are pleasing to see and not jumpy or confusing. Use a tone of voice that is confident and positive. The admissions people are looking for a good deal, just like everyone else who wants to "buy" something. Don't paint a picture that raises any questions about your quality.

Point of View

SUCCESSFUL ADS have a point of view. When an agency takes on a new product, it does massive, in-depth research on the product and the market. The ad agency knows that it can't tell the audience everything. There's not enough time or space for that kind of information saturation. An ad campaign narrows down its focus to several key points that need to be communicated and then designs the ad around those points. The college essay should be approached the same way. You've got to focus on a few key points that reveal who you are. You can't say everything. Five hundred words are more than you ever heard in a 60-second TV spot. But 500 words are still not enough to say *everything*. Don't squander this limited opportunity. Take a stand, and choose an approach that allows you to reveal who you are. Your life story is too long. Pick a few events, ideas, or values, and give your audience a clear, focused picture. Zoom in, focus, and run the camera. Don't make your essay a jump-cut production with a dozen scenes.

Hooks and Tags

THE AVERAGE national TV spot is a 60-second appeal to the market. The first words and images of the spot are the "hook," or lead, which brings the audience in and attempts to hold it for the body of the ad. The hook has to be something memorable and enticing, a statement that cries out for attention. Good leads in your college application essay perform the same function. They should be crafted to make the audience want to know more about you. A good hook should be easy to read and understand, yet have the ability to lead the reader into the information that follows. Lead sentences in paragraphs should not be long-winded or present arguments that can't be resolved within a few sentences.

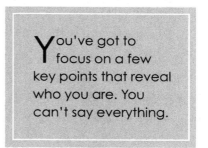

You've got to focus on a few key points that reveal who you are. You can't say everything.

Good leads are often just simple and true statements that require brief explanation and little detail.

An ad's "tag," or finish, is just as important as the hook for achieving impact and creating a favorable memory of the product. The final sentence, or "clincher," in a paragraph is a tag. It completes the thought of the paragraph and ties up all the

The first words and images of the spot are the "hook," or lead, which brings the audience in and attempts to hold it for the body of the ad.

points of the paragraph with a solid thought. Most successful tags are reflective. They look back on the material presented in the paragraph and make a statement that communicates a conclusive opinion or final result based on the logic of what has been expressed. The final sentence in your essay has a great responsibility. It must look back over the entire concept of the essay and say something that finishes the thought with conviction. A tag can't be "wimpy" or indirect. It should be a clear opinion that is proven without question by what has been written in the previous paragraphs. The tag should always be short and solid, never long, wordy, or complex. It is the last touch and the final shot. Your final sentence should strive for impact and closure, as does the last sentence in each of the following advertisements.

For Budget Rent-a-Car, 1990 (an ad appearing in an in-flight magazine):

We'll give you a reason to change rental cars in midair.

Got a deal on a rental car? Great. Bring it to Budget and we'll do anything to beat it. Like throwing in a better car or a bigger car for the same price. All you have to do is ask and we'll give you a better deal. Our wide selection of quality cars is subject to availability and these deals can't be reserved in advance. This offer is for walk-up customers only, so head straight for the Budget counter as soon as you land. It could be the best idea that ever came out of a blue sky.

A great price is just part of the deal.

An ad for *Time* magazine in 1976:

The soaps are like Big Macs . . . a lot of people who won't admit it eat them up.

Academic amnesia, vicarious VD, hypothetical hysterectomies: the world of TV soap opera. But Time *readers are among the least avid watchers of daytime television. Why was* Time *inspired to devote a cover story to TV soap opera?*

Because Time *readers are also insatiably curious* Time *probed the hypnotic appeal of the soaps, found a whole subculture, discovered the iron hand behind the wet handkerchief. And in so doing,* Time *demonstrates once again the rewards of analyzing seriously what seems on the surface to be egregious frivolity.*

You know what *Time* does. And reading it each week reminds you how well.

Both the Budget ad and the *Time* magazine ad adhere faithfully to the fundamentals of advertising copy. The leads are short, strong statements. There is no beating around the bush. They both speak with a purpose to an idea that will be developed quickly in the ensuing copy. The Budget ad uses a lead that addresses the reader directly. The tone is conversational and simple. It delineates *what* it's going to do and then develops the idea with an explanation of *how* it plans to execute the deal. Its tag uses a metaphor that connects the airport deal with the cliché about "blue-sky ideas."

The strength of the *Time* ad is in its lead and the copy that underscores it. The lead is a combination of a shock lead and a declaration that must be proven to survive. It is a smart way to start a paragraph because it draws you in to see what will happen with this bold assertion. You're hooked. The body of the ad then supports the contention with a stream of visual evidence, hard facts, and a question tag that forces you to the next paragraph. The tag line at the end isn't a knockout, but these ingredients can be put to equally good use in your college essay.

In 1952, Ernest Hemingway wrote an ad for Ballantine Ale. (Yes, nothing is sacred.) Hemingway, the ultimate minimalist, demonstrates here what ad copy always strives to create: quick communication of ideas, a good lead, images that make the copy "live," and a short, direct final punch.

> *Bob Benchley first introduced me to Ballantine Ale. It has been a good companion to me ever since.*
>
> *You have to work hard to deserve to drink it. But I would rather have a bottle of Ballantine Ale than any other drink after fighting a really big fish.*
>
> *We keep it iced in the bait box with chunks of ice packed around it. And you ought to taste it on a hot day when you have worked a big marlin fast because there were sharks after him.*
>
> *You are tired all the way through. The fish is landed untouched by the sharks and you have a bottle of Ballantine cold in your hand and drink it cool, light, and full-bodied, so it tastes good long after you have swallowed it. That's the test of an ale with me: whether it tastes as good afterwards as when it's going down. Ballantine does.*

The purpose of these illustrations is to display the ingredients that work well in ad copy. Even in a nearly fifty-year-old piece by Hemingway, the elements are the same. Pictures, easy delivery, and solid leads and tag lines. If your college application essay tries to say too much and lacks visual life, it will lose the attention of the admissions people who read it. Choose a direction and develop it simply. Give us leads that are easy to understand and flesh them out with images that support the main idea of the paragraph. Don't stray. Stay with the campaign you've designed for each paragraph. Finish with a statement that is strong, determined, and brief. The only thing that is more important in creating an impact than the first impression is the last impression.

In this chapter I do not mean to suggest that your college application should be an advertisement. I hope to impress upon you the fact that certain similarities apply to both ad copy and your essay. The communication techniques that you use to create the image of you that is most appealing, emotional, and likeable are much like those that ads use to create a warm feeling about their products. Take the most basic and honest direction—write the slice-of-life essay that reveals your values and beliefs. Madison Avenue has provided us with some marvelous advertising gimmicks, ideas, and directions, but none will ever be as effective as the story that is true and comes from the heart. There is no replacement for the truth told with insight and deep conviction.

Strategy Notes

Copy, Copy, Copy. Start a short file of your favorite print ads. Photocopy the ads and do a copy breakdown of the language used. Ask yourself, "Why does the ad work?" Then, write an ad for yourself, imitating the style of the ads you like. Describe the photo you would use to sell yourself and then imitate the types of syntax (word order) in each sentence of the ad copy. Experiment with the ad strategies. Use the voice, tone, and pace of the ad copy, just changing the product. This is a great way to learn how to write leads and body copy in your essay and will also get you to start thinking in a new and different way about words.

Gut Check. Are you expressing any emotions in your profiles or essay drafts? To find out, do a "gut check" and underline any sentences where you describe (not just talk about) feelings you've

Finish with a statement that is strong, determined, and brief.

had. If you are distancing yourself from real feelings in your essay, you're blowing a major requirement for any successful essay or advertisement. Lose the "talking heads" and tell the reader how you feel, what your experiences feel like, and tap into those emotions by using details that are alive. If you want to *live* in the essay, then you've got to show us that you're not a one-dimensional, marble statue. Have a heart!

Camera! Action! Here's an activity—one I use in my workshops—to challenge your cinematic imagination. Assume you've been given $150,000 to make a documentary film about yourself. It's a short documentary, about fifteen minutes in length, but that's more time than they'd give you on *60 Minutes* or *20/20*. The film, titled *Me,* is written, produced, and directed by you. As a bonus, you have the power to "time travel" and shoot any shots of your life that you'd like to have in the film.

Picture this: The audience sits in a darkened theater. The title comes up with principal credits, and then the screen fades into the opening scene of your film. What would we see in the first three-minute scene? Now, write the term *Fade In:* in the upper right-hand corner of a page and describe in the present tense what we see on the screen in vivid detail, from beginning to end of your first scene. Think like a camera, a film writer, a director. Show us the action. On another sheet of paper, write the final scene of your film. This is a two-minute scene, also described in the present tense from a fade-in, but this time there should be a final line of dialogue that reflects on the life of you, the subject of the film—in other words, last shot, last comment. This is a very effective activity that can open up an alternative writing style for you. I've seen some great paragraphs written as openings and closings in college essays that began with this exercise. Give it a shot.

5

Do's and Don'ts

You know that your college essay is serious business. It will help if you know the essential ingredients for a successful essay as well as the things you should avoid when you write it. Here are some dos and don'ts to consider before you put your essay together.

Be Positive and Upbeat

Occasionally the stress of applying to college gets the best of students; that stress seems to find its way into the essay portion of the application. Certain individuals use the essay to explain why their grades aren't as good as they could have been or why the SAT doesn't really measure their ability. Some students write apologies for their academic record or complain about their life in high school, spending the precious space in the essay to focus on a negative image of who they are. This strategy is a drastic mistake. It is counterproductive and results in an essay that

> The best way to present yourself in the essay is to accentuate the positive.

whines in a voice that destroys any positive elements in the student's folder.

The best way to present yourself in the essay is to accentuate the positive. The essay should present you in an upbeat way and avoid negative attitudes such as complaint and apology. As you discovered in chapter 3, there are many aspects about you that are unique and special. These are the elements in your personality and character that speak most forcefully on your behalf. Admissions officers don't want to hear about your emotional problems or detailed excuses that explain why your teachers didn't understand you. And even if they are legitimate examples of your growth, long stories of bad experiences can cast a shadow over your personality by dwelling too long, for instance, on the death of a friend or some other tragedy. There are better ways to express your honest grief and what you learned from it than exposing it in your college essay. You have to remember that the admissions committee is looking for someone who is going to add a positive influence to their college community.

Of course, the mention of a sad moment that expresses your compassion, the understanding of a wrong that should be righted, or the ability to change a habit that was thwarting your progress can help your cause if you deal more with the benefits of the experience than the gruesome details or painful wrenchings of your soul when things were bad. Try not to get into an area of tragedy or personal flaw.

Tell Us a Story

EVERYONE LOVES stories. They entertain us, captivate us, capture our imaginations like nothing else. The cultures of every people on earth are tied to their stories. If we lose our stories we lose our connection to our legacy as humans, both as members of our tribes and as individuals. The entire history of the planet is nothing more than a collection of stories, and the great books are all stories. Let's face it. If your college application essay doesn't tell a story in one way or another, you're sunk. It's a fact. What this means is that you must use the techniques of good stories in your essay.

Good story technique involves several key features that you've probably heard a great deal about from your literature teachers. For our purposes, we should look at the absolute necessities for a good story. Setting is vital—always tell us where the story is occurring and with as much sensory detail as is needed to make it "come alive" for us. Characters are always crucial. Tell us who is with you in your story and describe them—by name and with some identifying characteristics. You would be amazed at the number of times that students write a narrative paragraph in their essay and neglect to tell us who else is in the story. Stories should have action—important events that we can see and feel and that move the story along. Ernest Hemingway had a good piece of professional advice for young writers of narrative that can help any college application essay writer. He said, "Never confuse movement with action." In our application essay narratives, that can mean using an editorial touch to depict only the most important plot points of the story, avoiding unimportant events that fail to move the tale along. Every good story has a voice—the storyteller's voice that should be carefully crafted. When you tell a story in your essay, think of yourself as an actor narrating the tale that you are in or have witnessed and make certain that your voice has an attitude—a tone of respect, excitement, or mystery, amusement, perhaps, or even self-deprecation or incredulity. Whatever it may be, your story should have attitude. Finally, your story should be strategic—it must have a thematic truth that becomes evident by the close of the essay. (See chapter 7 for some samples of essays that succeed or fail to use story in an effective manner.)

Find a Coach or Editor

BEHIND EVERY great writer is an editor. The work of writing is such a personal endeavor that when you write, you need someone to tell you if you're getting through or just paddling around going nowhere. An editor or coach can act as an impartial judge, indicating if you're coming across loud and clear or if your message is garbled. You can save yourself a tremendous amount of trouble if you choose a knowledgeable, candid editor to look at your essay after you've written a good draft.

Find someone who understands what the college essay is supposed to be. Give your mentor a copy of this book and ask that he or she read a few chapters *before* reading your essay. Make sure that you choose someone who knows you but isn't afraid to tell you the truth about what you've written. You don't need strokes at this point—you need honest feedback from someone who reads more than the sports page and who's aware of the importance of this college essay.

Who do you ask? A good teacher or counselor might be a good choice. A wise parent can be a godsend, but make sure your parent has read this book so you will be certain that your editor has an informed perspective. It is okay to show your essay to good friends to see their reaction, but take great care about placing too much responsibility in their hands for a final judgment of your work. They are close to you, but will they have the objective touch that any good editor or coach has to have to

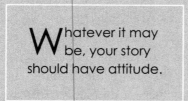

Whatever it may be, your story should have attitude.

help you with valuable advice? My suggestion is that you try to get to the English teacher, journalism instructor, or speech coach at your high school. If you can corner the chairperson of the English department or the best teacher on campus, that's even better. You know best whom you can trust to give you an honest evaluation, so use your good judgment here.

Before you write the essay, when you are going through the preliminary processes of choosing a topic, contact your editor or coach and ask if he or she would be willing to check your essay when you're ready to present it. Once you've got a commitment from a reliable mentor, continue your work. When you've finished a draft that you think needs feedback, submit it to your editor, typed and clean, with your copy of this handbook. Understand that your coach or editor is a busy person, and allow plenty of time for her or him to go over your essay. Ask about the most convenient time to go over the essay after he or she has read it. Set a firm date to meet with this person to discuss the essay.

When you meet with your coach or editor, listen carefully to what you hear. Have a duplicate of your essay with you so you can go over the copy together, making notes on your copy as you discuss the content, delivery, and anything else about the essay. If the editor has corrections or comments, write them down on your duplicate, even though he or she may have made notes on the essay copy you originally submitted. Tell the person clearly what you're trying to communicate in your essay so he or she can tell you whether you're reaching your objectives. An hour of the mentor's time for this first draft (not a *rough* draft, but a first, finished draft) should be long enough. Then go back and work out the bugs, if any exist.

Don't take the mentor's criticism personally—use it. If you think that he or she is wrong, save your opinion for yourself. You *did* ask for the mentor's opinion and should take whatever you get with gratitude for the attention you've received, despite whatever differences in opinion may arise.

After you've made the necessary adjustments on your copy, using and discarding what you choose of the mentor's advice, it's a good idea to give this person a final copy of your essay to read before you send it. Explain that you'd appreciate a "proofing" on your essay. Always write a thank-you note to your mentor (or give him or her a small gift, if you have the inclination). "Thank you" can be said in many ways, but it should never be something you let slide or forget, especially when the mentor has given time and advice to you.

Be Tasteful

IN 1988 the *Los Angeles Times* ran a front-page feature on college admissions, focusing its attention on a well-known private college that was very tough to get into and swamped with applicants. One of the elements of the story dealt with a top student applicant from the East who had everything going for him—grades, Board scores, "the works." The director of admissions described how this ace student wrote himself into a "self-destruct" mode with his college essay by writing about the many ways in which condoms may be used, technique and style included. Not only did the student not get into this prestigious college (which he must have thought would be hip to his sense of humor), but he received a reprimand from his headmaster and a demand for a written apology from the college after his prep school administration was contacted by the director of admissions.

Simply put, questionable taste is a dumb strategy for your essay. The old "gross out" may be funny in *Animal House* or *American Pie,* but it's not going to get you into a college if you try it in your essay, no matter how funny or talented a comic you may be. Save it for the fraternity if you must, but leave any disgusting references, sexual innuendoes, or sick jokes out of your essay. Admissions committees are looking for people with good taste and sound judgment. Exercise both of these in your essay and you'll be doing yourself a service.

Keep It Simple

THE QUALITY of your thought process, the choices you make, and how you deliver the material will do more for you than a massive dose of ideas and facts about you.

Keep your essay simple, clear, easy to read, and uncluttered with irrelevant material. Pick a few strong ideas and develop them. You can't say everything in the essay—there isn't room for it in 500 words (the maximum you should allow yourself). The admissions committee has neither the time to read a biblical account of your life nor the stamina for a long, complex story. They really appreciate the clear, the simple, and the concise. It shows them that you have a sense of what is important and the discipline to limit yourself to the essentials of good communication. Quality, not quantity, is the key here. It's true for just about everything . . . especially your essay.

To Thine Own Self Be True

PROBABLY ONE of the most disastrous things you can do in your essay is to try to sound like someone other than yourself. The essay is supposed to reveal *you,* and if you drag out the thesaurus for every other word or use language that isn't personal and real, your essay will sound contrived and phony. Your temptation to impress the admissions people with your articulate use of the English language can get you into trouble. The most effective essays are almost conversational in tone, delivered in the voice of the student. A relaxed sense of yourself and what you believe is far more forceful than the use of $50 words from the SAT vocabulary list.

A relaxed sense of yourself and what you believe is far more forceful than the use of $50 words from the SAT vocabulary list.

In my seminars I tell students that they should tape-record their essay and listen to it a few days later. Does the essay sound like you? If it doesn't, then your credibility will be in jeopardy and the essay will sound like an attempt to impress rather than communicate the essence of who you are. Consider this: Have you ever heard someone at a party who was trying to impress someone with his or her knowledge by saying things that were haughty or contrived? It makes you want to scream, right? Well, if you try to use a flashy vocabulary that isn't you, the admissions committee will pick it up in an instant. They are professionals and they read hundreds of essays. They are also real people, and they know how real individuals communicate. Save the vocabulary marvels for the SATs. The more your essay sounds as if a real person wrote it and the greater the degree of natural, flowing, honest thought in your language, the stronger your credibility will be.

Another important factor in respect to communicating the optimum essence of *you* in the essay is an ethical one. Tell the truth. Don't create a person who doesn't exist, try to inflate the facts, or invent situations that never happened. First of all, you don't *need* to invent anything about yourself, because you have many great things to discuss in your essay, as you can easily see from your profile worksheets. Second, you shouldn't start your college career by misrepresenting yourself in the application. People try it occasionally, and sometimes it comes back to haunt them.

A final note here is important: Write the essay yourself. Don't let your mom or dad write it—or anyone else, for that matter. There are individuals who will write the essay for you for a fee. (I've heard of one or two people in Los Angeles who charge several hundred dollars for this "service.") Not only is this dishonest, it is not going to do you any good. If you can't duplicate the writing skill of your ghostwriter in your classes, what is to stop a professor or teaching assistant from taking a look at your file and noticing that you were a great writer in the college essay but you can't communicate in English 1A? How will you explain that? It just doesn't pay to try and fake anything in the college essay. Be true to yourself and it will shine in the things you write.

Write It for Strangers

IF YOU write the essay with the attitude that whoever reads it does not know you at all and that this will make a first impression of you as a person, you will avoid one of the great pitfalls of weak writing. Many high school writers take their audience for granted and often leave key questions unanswered as they tell a story or express an idea. The questions that need clarification are simple ones: *who, what, where, when, why,* and *how.* When you proof your work, take care to see if these questions are clearly addressed and conveyed to the reader in every paragraph.

If you express an opinion in your essay, always support it with a reason, backed by experiences and examples that have led you to your point of view. When you mention specific people in your essay, briefly tell us something about them that tells *who* they are. An event that happened to you always has a setting (*where*). Give the strangers who read your essay a sense of place by way of a short description that locates the event. Never forget to tell us *when* something happened, especially if you're discussing a growth experience that took place in the past. Series of events should always be related to each other in a time frame. (How soon? How many months or days later?

How long before?) To tell us that something gave you a funny feeling and not say exactly *what* the feeling was like is leaving too much up to the reader. Don't be vague about your ideas. Give them substance. As you describe a crucial accomplishment, action, deed, or undertaking, tell *how* you did whatever was done. Fill in the blanks because your reader doesn't know you and doesn't want to guess.

After you've written the first draft of your essay, take a look at it from a stranger's point of view. What would someone think about you who had never met you and who was reading this for the first time? What might some of your ideas suggest? Have you made yourself clear enough in your delivery so that nothing can be interpreted in any other way than what you intended? Are your opinions well supported? Are your statements solid enough to stand on their own, out of context, and still be understood?

Take control. Make sure that what you're saying can be well understood by anyone, anywhere, of any age or background. You never know who'll be reading the essay, so assume that anyone might.

Somebody Say Something!

A STORY without dialogue can leave much to be desired. Silent films were fine for awhile, but when the "talkies" came in 1928 legends crumbled and stars were born, more for what they had to say in a scene than merely how they looked. I always tell my students to make sure that someone other than the student says something in the essay, if at all possible. This doesn't mean that we need a long stream of dialogue in your essay. We do need someone in your narrative to say something that brings the piece to life. The fact that you can give us a line of dialogue from a past event in your life—a comment from your mom, dad, a grandparent, or any significant person who has struck a resonant chord with you—can point directly to your sensitivity to life experience.

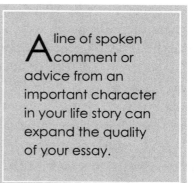

A line of spoken comment or advice from an important character in your life story can expand the quality of your essay.

My best advice here is to begin writing a list of things your family, friends, and teachers have said to you during your lifetime that you've always remembered, revered, or found compelling. As well, when you write a narrative, dig deep to recall something that was said that was a signature to the event. You know what we're looking for here, I'm sure. Think of how films often have those signature dialogue scenes that stay with us for years afterward, often only for a single line delivered at the right time by a key player. Your essay doesn't have to have a *Dirty Harry* line like, "A man's got to know his limitations," but a line of spoken comment or advice from an important character in your life story can expand the quality of your essay more effectively than you may realize. If the dialogue is delivered in a language other than English, always go with the original language and then explain what is said in the next sentence. The detail of a comment made in another language adds a fabric to your story that enriches it in many ways, but always translate the comment as soon as possible.

On Using Quotations

THE PROFILE section in Chapter Three discusses quotations at length, but this is more a cautionary reminder on the question of quotes. The words of others are too often overused in the college essay. The quote lead—starting your essay with a quote from a great mind or famous individual—is a very common technique in college essays. That's not to say that it isn't valid or that it won't be effective. It's just done often. If you are going to use a quote to start your essay, choose something that's a little different—a quote that is obscure, mysterious, or hilarious. Choose something with a meaning that will come to the reader as he or she reads your essay and not some preachy adage that he or she has already heard and that acts only as window dressing for your essay.

Whatever you choose, *don't* interpret the quote in your essay. Let the quote stand on its own if you use it at the beginning of your essay. The admissions committee people don't need you to explain the quote to them. They'll be more interested in how you *respond* to the quote lead than in your explanation of something that they can figure out on their own. Limit your use of quotes as well. The college wants to hear about you and your thoughts, not a litany of references to other people's words and ideas. Avoid the use of extended quotes, therefore, and ask your coach or mentor about the quotes you choose. Are they commonplace, trite, or overused?

An effective use of quotes can be to introduce the words of people you know personally who aren't famous or often quoted. The words of a parent, friend, or even a stranger you overheard in an elevator can be more interesting and make your essay unique. This kind of quote isn't secondhand and won't suggest that you're trying to impress us with words from Le Duc de la Rochefoucauld (who, by the way, does have some great quotes). It will be refreshing and show a sensitive use of this technique. A quote comes to mind that expresses the importance of handling the quote technique with great care:

> If you are going to use a quote to start your essay, choose something that's a little different—a quote that is obscure, mysterious, or hilarious.

In baiting a mouse trap with cheese, always leave room for the mouse. —Saki

Avoid Rock 'n' Roll

ROCK 'N' ROLL WILL never die, but spending a lot of time discussing your favorite band, however "together" they may be, as part of your college essay can be deadly. Some high school students find great inspiration in rock 'n' roll, and there's no denying that it may be legitimate in every way, but it's just not the right direction to take in the college essay. Chances are that it will be interpreted as frivolous and not serious enough to warrant the consideration of the admissions committee as the proper subject matter for the essay. Try to avoid rock stories, rock star encounters, and concert experiences in your essay. They seldom work and are hard to translate into language that an academic community can accept.

About Your Vacation . . .

VACATION STORIES in the college essay are like watching your Uncle Bert and Aunt Ethel's slides or videotapes of their trip to the Grand Canyon. You had to be there to really get the thrill. Vacation experiences are common in essays and most often are boring travelogue tales that don't say much other than to exclaim how great the trip was or how beautiful the buildings and people were. The only instances in which vacation stories seem to work are when the student discovers something from a particular incident on the trip that reveals something about himself or herself that is unique and significant. When a trip turns into a remarkable, personal learning experience and can be described briefly but in detail, it can be a strong statement for a student. The incident should be something specific and unique, and not just an overview of the culture or customs of a

SCARY TOPICS
WORTH AVOIDING

Approach these topics with caution:

- Your summer session at "Hotshot Prep" or "Lucky U."
- How wonderful your friends are
- The meaning of love
- Overcoming grief for one who has died
- Anything that deals with the yearbook work you did or being on the staff of the magazine or school paper (Your internship with a professional paper is, conversely, a good topic if you can demonstrate what you learned.)
- Your winning touchdown, basket, or spike in any big game
- Why "X" university is perfect for you and you for it (unless the college asks you to respond to this type of question)
- Your body (or anyone else's)
- Apologies or explanations of your academic record

particular place. Such a personal experience works far better than a litany of places you went to see and how impressed you were by the experience in general terms.

Scary Topics

SOME OTHER topics worth avoiding in the essay, either because they are typical and usually lack the imaginative force of more personal, unique experiences and ideas or because they are inherently dangerous due to their subject matter, can be found in the above sidebar.

- Anything criminal or unseemly, no matter what you learned

- A nervous breakdown or any mental illness (This is a private matter between you and your doctor and should remain that way.)

- What you think of someone else (The essay is about you and not another person.)

- How you plan to change the world

- Any conclusions that equate education with making money

- Blaming anyone for your circumstances, personal or academic

- Deep, long-winded exclamations of your religious or political beliefs

- Why the essay is so hard to write

- Anything violent or gruesome

Your profile is filled with unique and special events that happened *only* to you. The essential force in the essay that you always want to harness is the spirit that drives *your* life. The list of topics to avoid will help you steer clear of trite and commonplace, sometimes even maudlin and counterproductive, subjects. One yardstick to use to measure the acceptability of your topic choices is this one:

Would this be a topic I could have someone read aloud to an audience of a thousand people while I sat alone on the stage with a spotlight aimed right on me?

The Slings and Arrows of Outrageous Grammar

THE MECHANICS of your English are crucial. It's too late to try to teach you an entire course on English grammar at this point, but there are some typical errors you can avoid in your essay. Here are the grammatical and stylistic problems that you can look for as you proof your work. Their absence will make your copy clear, readable, and mature.

Topic Sentences

This area is covered extensively in chapter 6, but it deserves a cautionary mention here. Make sure that each of your paragraphs has a solid topic sentence and that all the other sentences in the paragraph are strictly devoted to developing that topic sentence. Don't ramble around and lose focus. Stay with the direction of each topic sentence.

Stranded Pronouns

Writers often seem to have a tough time with pronouns. People demand far too much from these little words, expecting them to be easily identified long after the word they are representing was mentioned. "It" and "they" are probably the most abused of the pronouns. These two pronouns are often used over and over again in an essay, leaving the reader quite confused in regard to which "it" the writer is referring, and which "they" is doing whatever is being done. The law of diminishing return is well applied to the use of pronouns in writing. The law states that the

> The essential force in the essay that you always want to harness is the spirit that drives *your* life.

more something is used, the less value it will have. The more a pronoun is used, the less meaning it will convey. Also, the farther a pronoun is from its antecedent, the less identifiable it is. When proofing your work in first draft, why not circle every pronoun and see if it is easily understandable and if it refers clearly to the idea you are using it to represent? If the pronoun is even the least bit vague, replace it with a synonym for the word it was carrying on its back.

Repetitious Usage

Check each sentence in your essay for words that are repeated. Nothing is more irritating than to read someone's writing and see the same word repeated at the outset or close of every other sentence. It not only shows lack of imagination, poor proofing skill, and limited use of vocabulary but also becomes very boring. Go through every sentence in your draft and underline the first and last word in each. See if certain words are popping up a great deal. Change your sentence structures if they are, and change the repeated words as well.

Another trap into which students frequently fall—one that makes their writing monotonous—is the subject-verb-object trap. In this common pattern, every sentence starts with a subject and goes from verb to object, over and over again. It results in choppy delivery and is especially bothersome when the student continuously uses the verb *to be* in some form, in the same pattern (e.g., I am, I did, I was . . .). Check your work for this kind of repetitious use of sentence structure and try to say what you mean in a less monotonous way. Keep your delivery natural but play with the order of the words a little. Interject a prepositional phrase occasionally, start the sentence with a gerund, or combine two sentences into a compound sentence. If you vary your sentence structure from one sentence to the next with an ear to the different rhythms of thought that you

Keep your delivery natural but play with the order of the words a little.

create, your essay will have a more dynamic delivery and be far more enjoyable for the people who read it.

Parentheses

Try to avoid using parentheses too often. (It's dumb.) Some people think that parentheses are a hip way to avoid transitions in sentences. (They're not.)

Misplaced Commas, Quotation Marks, and Semicolons

Commas, periods, and other forms of punctuation are, in many ways, signposts for how to breathe when reading a sentence. They are directions for delivering the words in a specified way. Periods get a breath and a pause. Commas get a brief breath, and semicolons are a breath without a long pause. If this sounds strange, try reading a paragraph without punctuation. Unless you're an underwater swimmer who can hold your breath for five minutes, you can turn blue in about four sentences. If you quote someone in your essay, you must put the quotation marks at the beginning and end of what they say. And be sure to tell who said what by setting off the quotations from the rest of the text with a comma (usually inside the quotation marks). Your readers hear what *they* say, see that *you* didn't say it and that *they* did, and get a breath while they think about it.

If you have problems with punctuation, think about sound and breath; then read the essay into a tape recorder the way you want it to sound. Listen to the replay and follow along with your copy. Punctuate according to the way each sentence sounds to you as you hear the playback. If you missed a pause for a comma, put one in, and if your sentences sound too long, break them up with punctuation. When people read anything, a little voice in their head sounds out the words and breaths, even if they are speed readers but especially if they read for style and delivery, as admissions officers do. Your coach or editor can help you with your use of punctuation.

Exclamation Points

Listen! Avoid too many exclamation points in your sentences and use them only when something happens that is truly excitable and amazing. Look out! Too many of these !!! can make your work seem very immature.

Abbreviations

Don't abbrev. anywhere in your essay.

Prepositions

Don't end sentences with a preposition. Always give every preposition an object.

Tense

Don't give your readers "time whiplash" by shifting from past to future, to present, to future, and back to the past. Think about the film *Back to the Future II,* and you can appreciate the problem of shifting tenses.

Work with your coach to check for these and other grammatical inconsistencies as you proof your drafts.

Get to the Point

YOU DON'T have the luxury of unlimited space in the essay and admissions officers read dozens of essays per day, so you have to grab their attention quickly. Don't spend valuable time in endless explanations or long descriptions of things that aren't about *you.* If you follow the profile through to its completion, you will find several areas of your life that you can address quickly in the essay and that will move your audience into your topic. Look back to your profile. Good sections in which to find material for introductory paragraphs are sections 1, 5, 11, 12, 21, and 25. You can obviously choose any material that feels like a good place to start, but it is important to involve the audience immediately in the subject of the essay, which is *you*.

Significance Is Significant

JUST BECAUSE you say that something has great meaning for you is not enough. When an event moves you, a person has had a tremendous impact on your life, or a particular belief has made the difference in your personal perspective, you must tell *why* this and other elements in your growth history have significance to you.

A college education is a process that is welded together by a search for meaning. The significance of events, ideas, and beliefs is the ground upon which most college courses are built. In order to demonstrate your readiness and maturity for this kind of discipline, you must show some awareness of the significance of things, people, events, and ideas in your own life, and you should express your understanding of the meaning of some important facets of your life. Don't just make declarations and leave the audience to figure out why something is important. Tell the reader why a moment or a person or a particular belief has significance to you.

Skip the Hearts and Flowers

OVERDOING DESCRIPTIVE language, flowery and cluttered imagery, and usage that is archaic or unnatural can "do you in" as you write your essay. Again, the essay should sound like a real person is writing it, not someone who is addicted to adjectives and to the constant pairing of verbs with adverbs in an effort to prop up the verbs. You just don't speak that way, and you won't get through to the admissions committee in your essay if your technique stands in the way. Try to avoid endlessly long sentences—even if

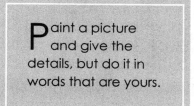

Paint a picture and give the details, but do it in words that are yours.

they are grammatically correct. They will seem windy and can become very boring. Be yourself. Paint a picture and give the details, but do it in words that are yours. If you rely on the thesaurus too often and use words and phrases that are not you, your readers won't get a sense of the *person* in the essay.

On Writing Those Short Essay Topics

IN THE last five years or so, a number of private colleges and universities have begun adding the short essay "question" to their menu of essay queries in the application. Frankly, these little essays are devilish creatures because they ask the applicant to fill a very confined space with pithy bursts of inspiration—a kind of hellish haiku of the application process.

How do you attack these questions or topics? Of course, it depends on the particular topic, but most of these prompts ask for little more than 150-word responses. (You *can* squeeze a few more words into the required space if you measure the space provided with dummy copy first and use a font that gives you more space to work with . . . but quality is more important than quantity here.) The topics range from little beauties like "Jot a note to your future roommate" to "Tell us about something you've always wanted to know," or "How would you solve 'X' problem" to "If you could hold any position of power in the national government which would you choose and why?"

Many students in my workshops and A.P. English literature classes ask me how to approach these shorter topics and I direct them to the power of short ad copy. These essays are

> The short essay almost begs for anecdotal narrative.

mostly style pieces. Every word counts, certainly, and that means the lead has to go right at the prompt with a direct, forceful impact. No long-winded sentence to start the short essay. Like a good boxer who wants to announce his presence in the ring, you've got to go out there and hit something quickly and with authority.

The short essay almost begs for anecdotal narrative, as well. Set up a situation in the problem solving essay prompts, using some sensory detail, and then solve the problem, discussing why you chose the solution. In those "Jot a note" prompts, tone is crucial—the college is looking for a descriptor of personality and originality. You don't want to lose sight of the fact that every essay is an opportunity to tell the university about something that is singularly *you*, so the "note" should be positive and personal in tone, revealing something that is important to you. It doesn't have to be a real-life note or confession. You needn't say the typical: "Hi, I'm Jane or Joe and I really can't wait to meet you, etc." Ouch! You might as well say "Hi! I have no imagination." You need to create a scenario in the note that allows you to converse with this unknown person.

Example: Assume you've already met; now invite them to do something fun with you and some of your friends. The idea is to think "How can I write this so that it's an advertisement of who I am and what I like, or what I think is important?"

On Answering the Question "Why Do You Want to Attend Lucky U.?"

FOR REASONS I will never understand, some of our private colleges insist on asking their applicants to answer this prompt with an essay. It has to be one of the most unrevealing questions one could imagine, simply because there are only a limited number of answers and the admissions committee has to read the same responses over and over. Is it possible that the university actually wants to hear thousands of applicants tell the committee that their school is "the number one college in America for me" from every kid who applies there? Do they really believe that their college is every applicant's number one choice? My advice to students faced with this foolish question is to do some research on the university and what it provides. I suggest that they interview a current student of the college or a recent alum, asking about what the place is really like, the traditionally popular programs, the names of the libraries and buildings, and campus traditions that everyone loves.

If the goal of the admissions office is to see how gung-ho the applicant is, then the best way to show them that you are is to really know the university for its cherished traditions and that means writing an essay with some attention to intimate details. This should be an automatic course of action if the college actually is your number one choice. From school colors, whether they be Hoya blue and gray or Irish blue and gold, to dropping names of famous grads or ivy-covered buildings and time-honored trivia—a question like this one demands more than patent generalities about the great rep that the college has and how beautiful the campus is. And, the tone should be reverent, as if the school fight song were being sung *a capella* in the background as we read your essay.

Never Say . . .

HERE'S A list of things that you should avoid writing in your essay. There are a thousand reasons to avoid them, most of which are obvious. But the most important reason is that they don't work *for* you but against you.

NEVER SAY

WHY

+ In conclusion . . .

—It's amateurish, boring, and common.

+ Anything bleepable

—Obviously.

+ Rad, bitchin', cool, buzzkill, neat, bad, totally awesome jammin', etc.

—Especially if you really mean it.

+ Anything that can get you arrested

—Regardless of what you learned or how sorry you are. Tell your parents or turn yourself in to the authorities, but don't blow your shot at college with a confession of a bad deed.

+ That you wrote the essay the night before the deadline.

—Unless it is really *that* good.

+ However . . .

—More than once.

+ Etc., etc.

—Don't make us guess what the et cetera might mean.

+ Anything sexual

—Please.

+ That you don't care

—The admissions committee will believe you

+ That you're applying to "X" University because your boyfriend/ girlfriend is going there

—This is not *Love Connection* or *Change of Heart.*

+ That you're looking forward to college parties and fraternity or sorority events because of what you've heard

—This is not *Animal House.*

✦ Something untrue	—It's wrong and unethical and you may get caught. It can happen.
✦ That you hate anyone	—Hatred is the demonstration of a closed mind.
✦ That you wish you were different, or better, or smarter	—Accentuate the positive and don't beat up on yourself.
✦ That you're in it for the money	—Not an admirable motivation in the eyes of the university. And it's crass and common as well.
✦ That your parents don't understand you or your friends	—Nobody's parents understand them or their friends all the time.
✦ That anything "sucks"	—Even when it does.
✦ That someone helped you write the essay	—Don't let anyone write your essay . . . please.
✦ That you don't know why you think or feel the way you do	—Ever . . . in the essay.

Keep It Short

DON'T GO beyond the usual 500-word maximum. When you write the essay and limit yourself to a particular number of words—most colleges ask for 350 or 500 words—you demonstrate your discipline and ability to follow directions. If you go beyond the expected limit, you also make the reading a chore for the admissions officers, who don't want a long account of your life and times. Don't turn the essay into a long job for them and you'll be appreciated. Less is more in this respect.

Your essay should be a pleasure to read and not hard work for overworked admissions people.

Dumb, Dumber, and Dumbest

"Uh, Does Spelling Count?" My wife, Jacqueline, is an admissions officer for a major university. She occasionally shows me essays that strike her in one way or another, and some of them are remarkably well written. However, far too often there are people who submit essays that are rife with spelling errors, run-on sentences, and sentence fragments. I once read an essay that literally had 32 spelling errors on the first page—an automatic rejection! Proof your work, and not just with spell check. Get someone who can spell to read your essay before you mail it.

"Uh, Beavis? Mail This, Okay?" How would you feel if you got a valentine from your favorite person with the salutation delivered to somebody else? Sad, right? Well, the number of students who send the wrong essay to the wrong college is significant enough to mention that you don't want to mix up your essays because you're stressed about the deadline. This is an automatic rejection in many instances. Triple-check to make sure that the right essay is going into the correct envelope.

"Uh, What?" Don't forget to write your name (and any other required information) on each page of your essay. To avoid confusion for the admissions officers, make sure the pages are stapled in order. Type your essay (unless the college asks you to do otherwise). Don't cross out words and handwrite them in. Don't use white-out—type it again or print out a new, clean copy. Do people actually forget and do these things incorrectly? Yes! And some of them don't get into the college of their choice because of these dumb mistakes. "Right, Beavis?" . . . "Uh . . . yeah . . . sure dude."

6

It's Showtime!

Lost for words? The first sentence is always the toughest. Even when a writer thinks that there is something very important to say and that it must be written, there is that intimidating blank page staring back, waiting and daring someone to fill it with words that will be worth reading. Stories about writer's block, that dreaded condition that afflicts the writer with complete paralysis, are not myth. It has been said that when Ernest Hemingway was stricken with writer's block in midcareer, he would defrost his refrigerator and sit in the kitchen listening to the ice thaw until the words came to him. Dorothy Parker, one of America's great humorists, would quit smoking, a habit she enjoyed to excess, until the ideas would come. No one has the cure for writer's block, but anyone who has had to write anything of importance knows a little of what it must feel like. The blank page just glares in defiance at you from the typewriter, or the screen on your computer glows in blue-green, humming perhaps, the cursor blipping in time, impatient, as if to say, "What's the matter? Brain not working today? Are you too lame to have anything worth reading?" It's awful, I know. But, there are ways around this very common problem. You have to reach back to kindergarten for the basic tool that can lift you out of this predicament.

Kindergarten was a long time ago, and it probably doesn't seem like it has very much to do with your college application essay but, in fact, it is going to be crucial to your writing. Back in kindergarten there was an exercise that asked children to show and tell. You might recall the ritual. Every child is asked to bring something from home, an object of some significance—a toy perhaps, or a tool or a picture. The point of the procedure is to show the other kids the "thing" and then to tell them about it in his or her own words. Usually the student will show the class what the thing is and then describe what it does and what it means and maybe even elaborate about the thing by explaining a particular story that is related to it. As in any communication, the content of the story is determined by two key elements: what the thing is and what the thing means. Show and tell . . . it's simple.

Most effective writing conforms to the same rules that are used in show and tell. Occasionally the order of the process is reversed and it becomes "tell and show," but the idea is still the same. If you remember this very useful approach to communication, you'll have far more success in your writing, whether it's the college application essay, a law brief, a marketing report, advertising copy, or a movie script. In the college application essay, both description—the "show"—and significance—the "tell"—are indispensable. Both of these aspects have to be balanced. Too much "tell" or too much "show" can cause your writing to be boring and misleading. The one thing you never want to do when you are communicating is to give the audience too much of a picture or description without telling them the significance of the "show." In the other direction, don't talk forever about meaning and concepts without giving the audience a picture of your idea, an illustration that makes the idea something they can see. A good rule in all communica-

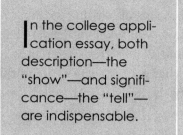

In the college application essay, both description—the "show"—and significance—the "tell"— are indispensable.

tion is to balance an idea with an illustration of what you're telling and, likewise, balance a description of an event, moment, place, or thing with an explanation of the significance of what it is you've described to the audience. This is especially important in the college application essay because your understanding of meaning and significance gives evidence of your scholarly perspective. Your ability to back up ideas with evidence also illustrates your understanding that thoughts without proof are flimsy thoughts.

Be aware of show and tell as you write this essay. This will help you avoid getting too involved with concepts, endless descriptions, and stories that don't connect clearly with ideas. If you stay in the show-and-tell spirit as you start to put the essay together, you will be on your way to a solid piece of writing.

The Tune-Up

THE WRITING process has three distinct phases that combine to create a final product: preparation, organization, and editing. Ignore any one phase and you risk a poor result. The first step is preparation, and you are well on your way to completing that. Your personal profile is detailed, and you have some solid information to use. Research into your background information is complete, and now you have the necessary information and momentum to empower you to make some choices.

Writing is about making choices. The second step in the process of writing is organizing your choices and deciding how you want to deliver them. Briefly go through chapters 1 and 2 to refresh your memory on who the audience is and what your objectives are in this essay. Write a short description of the essay as you see it in your own words and a brief description of admissions officers. Take control by identifying your objectives.

The third phase of the writing process is editing and revision of the rough draft. I will discuss this in detail once you've got something to edit and revise. Our goal at this point in the process is to start the actual writing. (Some writers call this drafting, and some teachers call it the composition phase.)

Drafting a written document demands that you look at all three phases even as you write the words. You have to look at the background material and make choices to accept or reject certain ideas as you write; you also must think ahead to the edit phase and avoid mistakes in organization that will have to be corrected later. It is important to remember that your first draft is not going to be perfect. Rewriting is just as much a part of the writing process as is thinking before you write. Now the important thing is to get something down on paper that you can form and mold to your liking.

Take Five

AT THIS point before you write the essay, it's a good idea to loosen up your brain a little by writing some unstructured thoughts that may or may not relate to the essay at all. This exercise is called free writing, and it works this way. Grab some paper and a pen. (Don't type your free writing—do it by hand.) Look at your watch. Give yourself five minutes to write anything and everything that comes to your mind about the essay, how you feel, what you're thinking about life, the day you may have had, your random thoughts, anything. You don't have to write sentences or brilliant ideas or paragraphs—just write. Blow out the valves in your brain and don't stop for even five seconds to think. Write freely, without structure or pressure to be smart or coherent. If confusion is your present state, write about it. If you're hungry, write about food. Just write freely. Do this for five minutes each night before you work on your college application essay to get your brain in a writing mode and to clear out the "garbage" that we all carry around in our heads before we can actually concentrate on something. Do it, please. It works, and it relieves stress. And don't throw it away when you're finished. You may find something in that jumble of thoughts that belongs in your essay. You never know.

Choices and Decisions

TAKE OUT your personal profile and read through it. Perhaps as you were working on each section of the profile, you liked certain things that you discovered or wrote. Pull out the material that you like, the sections that portray who you are. Look for ideas and images, stories and quotes that reveal something about you. They're in there somewhere. Try to limit yourself to five sections in the profile. Make some choices and then take a look at the five sections that you have pulled from the profile. Are there any elements in the rest of your profile that overlap into one of the five sections you chose? If so, write them out on a separate sheet and attach them to the appropriate section. Narrow down your approach to the essay in this way and it will begin to seem like an easier mountain to climb. You're in control and making decisions about what you want in your personal essay. When you've decided what you want the admissions officers to know about you, you are ready to write the essay.

The Huddle

IN THE game of football, strategy is all-important. Winning teams have several similarities, but the number of stars on a team or the size and strength of the players are only small factors in the difference between champs and chumps. The game is similar to what you have to accomplish in your essay. You will need a strategy that complements your material, much as a team needs to design its plays around its strength and talent. If you've scrutinized your research and determined what works for you, you've picked the players that are going to be used in your game plan. At this stage of the writing process, you have chosen what you want to say, in rough terms, and now you have to run some practice sessions to see how everything plays. You're not going to determine strategy just yet. You're going to run some ideas onto the field and see how they work. That means you'll write some isolated paragraphs that can stand alone without any connection to each other except for the fact that the topic of each paragraph is directly related to you. Just as with any team practice, first you'll warm up, as you have with the free writing exercise, and then you'll work on executing a few plays. A paragraph is exactly like a play in a football game. It has elements that have to be executed in a certain order, with precision and timing. Every sentence, like every player, has a job to do to accomplish the ultimate goal. In this case, the sentence has to relate to the goal of the paragraph, which is to gain ground on the topic.

> Every sentence, like every player, has a job to do to accomplish the ultimate goal.

For each section of the profile that you chose, write a paragraph that communicates *you* through the topic. How should you write the paragraph? If you assume you already know how to write a paragraph, you will make the kind of mistake that no decent coach would ever allow during a practice session. Just because the players know how to play the game does not mean that they ignore the "fundamentals" during practice. So let's look at the fundamentals of the paragraphs

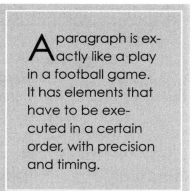

A paragraph is exactly like a play in a football game. It has elements that have to be executed in a certain order, with precision and timing.

you're going to write. Similar to the chalk-talk session before a play is put together on the field, let's run through how different paragraphs are executed.

Leads

THE BASIC paragraph in your college essay has to have "snap." Like a good play, it should open quickly and cleanly. Remember that the first sentence in a paragraph is called a *lead*. Knowing how to write a good lead for every paragraph in your college application essay is probably the single most important technical factor in your essay. Why? Some admissions officers have so many essays to read during the course of the admissions process that they read the first sentence of each paragraph before they read the essay from beginning to end to determine if they like the essay or not. They know that people who can't write solid leads usually write weak paragraphs. It saves them time, and they can breeze through your essay if they're tired of reading very closely, just looking at the leads and forming an opinion about the quality of your writing by simply reading the five or so leads that begin your paragraphs. Your leads must be good.

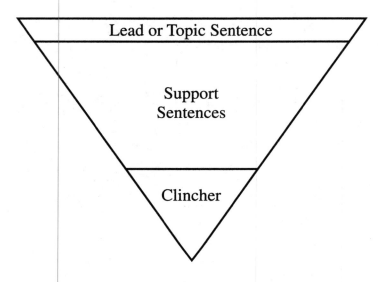

Figure 6.1   The Paragraph Pyramid

A paragraph is a unit of communication that moves from the general to the particular. In most cases, it works like an inverted pyramid, as illustrated in figure 6.1.

The top line of the inverted pyramid is the beginning of the paragraph, or the lead, and the remaining space inside the paragraph moves in an ever-narrowing area to a point at the small end of the pyramid. The pyramid starts as a broad visual image, as a paragraph should begin in general terms. As the pyramid moves downward to a specific point, so should a paragraph arrive at a specific point that is developed from a general statement. If you can picture the inverted pyramid as a metaphor for what a paragraph is supposed to do for your communication, you can understand how most leads start the "play" that a paragraph is attempting to execute.

The basic paragraph in your college essay has to have "snap."

Leads are like hook lines, or headlines, in advertising copy, as we discussed in chapter 4. They set up the information that's coming. Some leads—in fact, most leads—are topic sentences, but this is not true in every case. In the newspaper or journalism business, leads fall into two categories: standard leads and freak leads.

Standard leads are sentences that answer any one or a combination of six basic questions: *who, what, where, when, why,* and *how?* A summary lead is a sentence that tries to answer as many of these questions as it can in one sentence.

Who lead: David Bowie is one of rock music's great innovators.

What lead: Rock music has a major influence on young people throughout the world.

Where lead: Hollywood is a town that defies explanation.

When lead: Last week I learned that timing is everything.

Why lead: Johnny B. Goode played his guitar to win the heart of every Suzie Q. that he knew.

How lead: The best way to get ahead is to get started.

Summary lead: On December 8, in 1980, John Lennon was shot and killed by a crazed autograph seeker in The Dakota Building in downtown Manhattan, the assailant hoping to gain national prominence by committing the tragic crime.

The function of every one of these standard leads is to answer a particular question. Who is David Bowie? What has a major influence on young people worldwide? Why does Johnny play his guitar? And so on. Leads are the opening maneuver in each paragraph's "play"; the rest of the paragraph is supposed to follow through with more detailed information about the lead if the lead is the topic sentence.

The exceptions to this situation are those instances in which the lead is more a hook to set up the topic sentence that's coming next. These kinds of leads are usually called *freak leads,* because they do strange things to the reader and therefore hook the reader into the paragraph using various techniques that create interest.

The most effective freak leads are as follows: the *question* lead, the *stat* lead, the *quote* lead, the *shock* lead, the *suspended-interest* lead, and the *imperative* lead. These leads are very simple techniques for catching a reader's attention. They get the reader right into the paragraph without circling around the idea you're trying to communicate.

The *question* lead asks a question of the reader: What matters to me more than anything?

The *stat* lead gives the reader a statistic or fact that relates to the topic: I weigh 172 pounds and 6 ounces.

The *quote* lead obviously quotes someone saying something that relates to your topic: Vince Lombardi once told his Green Bay Packers at the start of a season, "If you're not fired with enthusiasm, you'll be fired with enthusiasm."

The *shock* lead says something that stuns the reader and entices the audience to read on for more information: Television is electronic heroin.

The *suspended-interest* lead leaves out important information and tempts the reader to go farther into the paragraph to discover the meaning of the opening sentence: He never gave up on me.

The *imperative* lead commands the reader to do something: Read this essay with an open mind.

Freak leads are a wonderful technique for getting the reader into your essay with energy. Like any device, however, they must be used with care. If you do a freak lead in every paragraph of your essay, you can appear to be too "cute" or manipulative, so it's important to be judicious in your use of these tools. The less-is-more rule of presentation is applicable here.

Your technique should never distract the reader from your content, but it should help the content to be delivered clearly.

The Paragraph

PICK A lead that will work for each of the five paragraphs you will write, remembering that any one of these paragraphs could be the opening paragraph of your essay. Each paragraph must be able to stand alone in a personal statement essay, so don't rely on one paragraph to help out another. Make each paragraph strong enough to say something about you strictly on its own. How do you do that? Follow your lead with support sentences that develop the topic. There are three methods that can be used to develop and support your topic in each paragraph. They are show-and-tell devices that create clarity for the reader. One is *detail*. Another is the use of *examples*. The third is *explanation*.

Let's take another look at the inverted pyramid, shown in figure 6.2.

The upper section of the pyramid represents the lead. If you've used a freak lead to start the paragraph, then the second sentence is your topic sentence. If you used a standard lead, then that's your topic sentence. A topic sentence is a general statement that needs to be supported with more information, such as examples, facts, or details. It demands expansion but states two things very clearly: what you're talking about, or the *subject* to be discussed, and the point of view (P.O.V.) or angle of approach on which you will zoom in as you discuss the topic. All topic sentences have both subjects and P.O.V.s that set the stage for what will follow.

Freak leads are a wonderful technique for getting the reader into your essay with energy.

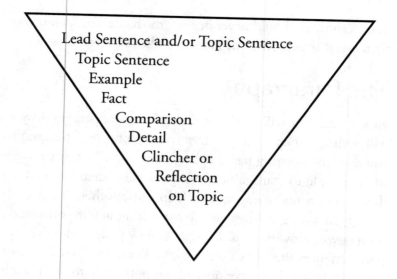

Figure 6.2 The Paragraph

For example: *My high school years were not easy ones, but they challenged me to grow.*

The subject here is "my high school years." The P.O.V, or focus, is "not easy" but "challenging."

These two elements now dictate what every sentence—*every sentence*—in the paragraph will discuss. You'll give details about hard work and difficulties during your high school years, examples of one or two real events that were not easy but that challenged you to grow. You'll explain how these events helped you grow and what you learned from the experiences. *Details, examples, explanation:* Use these three elements to develop and communicate the evidence that *proves* your topic sentence and clearly illustrates it.

We live in a highly visual time. We watch television, we go to the movies, we gawk at car accidents on the freeway, and we dress to be seen or to express our image. We even drive cars as if they were metal clothing that we wear to express who we are.

As a society we are locked into pictures. Paragraphs in your college application also have to be illustrative. There have to be pictures that illustrate you. Every topic sentence needs to have an illustration or example quickly attached to it. An anecdote that tells a story about the

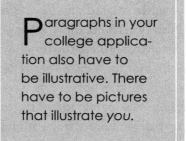

Paragraphs in your college application also have to be illustrative. There have to be pictures that illustrate *you*.

topic is a picture with a point. Instances, moments, and events all illustrate a particular topic. They are pictures. Use them to support your topic sentences.

Information is a basic necessity of life. You need information to live intelligently and succeed. Topic sentences need information, too. Detail in a paragraph is information that makes the audience know more about your topic. It helps them hold onto the important ideas with hard facts and real pictures that are more substantial than generalities. If you say, for instance, "I love to work with my hands," and this is your topic sentence, what must follow immediately is *detail* about *what* work you do with your hands, *why* you enjoy the work, *when* you do this kind of activity, *where* you do it, *how* you do the things that you do, and *what you learned* from this activity that illustrates your dedication, intelligence, inspiration, and understanding of yourself. Remember that this is a college application essay, and the admissions officers want to know what kind of student of life you are. Good students respect detail.

The use of detail in your paragraphs enriches your topic with substance and always answers the questions *what, how, where, when,* and—most important—*why.* The audience needs to know, and they'll be frustrated by you if you don't give them what they need.

Information and pictures that illustrate the topic are the essential ingredients of the middle of your inverted pyramid. Now, after you show what you tell in the topic sentence, you have to complete the process at the end of the paragraph with a "clincher" sentence, or "reflection statement." This final sentence in the paragraph is crucial. It is your chance to "nail down" the paragraph with authority, like a slam-dunk in a basketball game or a spike after a touchdown is scored.

The Spike

LIFE BEGINS with the hope of a happy ending, and many endeavors end with the hope of a new beginning. How we begin something often determines how we finish it. The satisfaction we feel after a good meal is directly related to how it was prepared at the beginning. A scene in a movie is successful because of many things: acting, direction, lighting, and editing, but the opening setup shot and the last shot will determine the *impact* that the scene has for the audience. The beginning and end have something in common and must relate to each other. Paragraph leads and clinchers have the same relationship. The last sentence in the paragraph must have a strong relationship to the beginning of the paragraph. It has to conclude the meaning of the paragraph with a statement that reflects back to the main idea. In the inverted pyramid illustration, the final sentence of the paragraph comes at the point of the pyramid. It is the point of the paragraph in many ways. Like a spike, it nails down the paragraph with a final point that reflects the main idea of the topic sentence.

The final sentence in a paragraph, the clincher, must finish the writer's thought. This can be the place for the writer to express an opinion about the main idea of the paragraph. A personal reflection can be ideal as the last thought in a paragraph, as demonstrated in the following example:

I dreaded my freshman year in high school. My brother, Nick, had just graduated from Madison High the previous year as an all-star football player and solid B student. He was a popular, all-world hero who had always been successful in everything he did. I can't count the number of times that I heard someone say, "This is Jimmy, Nick Brennan's little brother," during my first few weeks at school. For a while I tried to compete against my brother's ghost at Madison. I went out for football, and was cut. I ran for freshman class president, and I lost the election. I tried everything that Nick had ever done and failed miserably. **There is no more embarrassing failure than doing a bad job of being someone that you're not.**

> Like a spike, the final sentence nails down the paragraph with a final point that reflects the main idea of the topic sentence.

This kind of clincher is pure reflection and personal opinion. It looks back on an experience and states the writer's point of view about the events; it reveals a sensitive perspective that clinches the paragraph. Of course, there are other techniques that are used in the tag, or clincher, sentence. A question tag often sets up the next paragraph. A quote tag is usually used as a reflection on the content of the preceding sentences. Regardless of which type of tag you use in your essay, be aware that it must "clinch" the main idea of the paragraph and finish the thought with impact.

Getting Your Act Together

NOW YOU should have five paragraphs written that do the following things. Each can stand alone as a group of sentences that develop a central thought. The supportive sentences are visual, clear, and simple. Wherever a picture sentence appears, an explanatory sentence follows it. Wherever a concept appears, a picture sentence that illustrates the concept also logically follows soon after it. The lead sentence and tag sentence are designed to work for the paragraph and don't just "happen" at random because you decided to write whatever came into your head. Every paragraph you've written for your college application essay should be scrutinized this way. Think of the audience. Are you communicating with them in a way that keeps them with you all the way?

Now, take a look at the *pacing* of your sentences. Often, students write sentences that are of the same length. They don't "listen" to their work with an ear to the rhythm of the sentences and end up writing the same sound over and over again. This will destroy the audience's involvement in your work. It's death by boredom. The pace of your sentences can help your delivery be more interesting because it offers the reader a variety of "sounds." Sentence length paces your sentences in different ways.

There are three distinct sentence lengths: long, medium, and short. Long sentences are complex or compound sentences, often using phrases set off by commas or clauses that explain a thought in great length. They can be very effective in relaying a large amount of information in one thought. Summary leads illustrate this type of sentence. Medium sentences are usually complex or compound sentences that use dependent and independent clauses without becoming too detailed or lengthy. Short sentences are just that: short and to the point. They say what they

> The pace of your sentences can help your delivery be more interesting because it offers the reader a variety of "sounds."

must in a burst of subject, verb, and object—and they're over. Short sentences have great impact.

Before you write the final draft of each paragraph, try a simple pacing test to determine if your sentences have a variety of sounds. Number your long sentences with a 3, your medium sentences with a 2, and your short sentences with a 1. If you find that you have a series of 3s and 2s, then you need to break up this monotony with some short sentences that have impact. If you discover that you've written several 1s in a series, then your delivery is choppy and needs the variety of medium and long sentences. Combine some of the short sentences together as complex or compound sentences. A strong, well-paced paragraph should have pacing numbers that look like this: 1-3-2-2-3-1. A boring, monotonous paragraph will usually have numbers like this: 2-2-2-3-2-1-1-1-2-3. There are always exceptions to the pacing test. Some writers, such as Herman Melville in *Moby Dick*, write long, highly complex sentences that are nearly the length of paragraphs. They are beautifully constructed, classic prose and demand the attention of a reader who is ready for the long novel. These long sentences don't lend themselves well to the essay style, however. Essays call for more efficiency of language. You're trying to hold the attention of an audience that has read a hundred or more essays before they picked yours from the pile on their desk. Your pace should have energy and be dynamic. It should offer a variety and not a monotone or litany of long passages.

In chapter 3 you were asked to collect information and to write a paragraph for each of the items on the list. Several topics from that list can be used to create interesting lead paragraphs, solid paragraphs for the body of a personal essay, and paragraphs that can serve well to conclude your college application essay. To find good opening, middle, and concluding paragraph items from your personal profile, refer to the following guide:

GUIDE TO PARAGRAPH TOPICS

Beginning Paragraph Topics

Response to a quote (7)

Five things you know (9)

Your definition of happiness (10)

A memory of your parents (11)

A childhood memory (12)

Five special things about you (14)

Your one-sentence philosophy of life (15)

A description of yourself to a stranger (22)

Ten things you like and ten things you don't like (24)

A question you always wanted answered and why (26)

Middle, or Body, Paragraph Topics

A person or persons who have influenced you (1)

Virtues you admire (3)

A significant lesson learned (4)

A memorable experience (5)

A failure that taught you something (6)

If you have absolutely no idea how to organize your essay and need some kind of structure, this list of paragraph topics may help you narrow down the choices. This is *your* essay, and you can write about *anything* that you feel gives the admissions officers the best sense of who you are.

Perhaps the essay question from a particular college does not ask for a personal statement, but instead wants you to re-

Your greatest success (8)

A funny thing that happened to you (16)

A place that impressed you (18)

A favorite social activity (19)

A favorite intellectual activity (20)

A fear you conquered (22)

Concluding, or Final, Paragraph Topics

A goal you have in life (23)

What your friends say about you (25)

A question you always wanted answered and why (26)

What an education is supposed to provide (13)

What makes the world go around (17)

A quote that means something to you (7)

Five things that you know (9)

Your definition of happiness (10)

Your one-sentence philosophy of life (15)

spond to a specific question or assignment. If this is the case, you have several options.

Specific essay questions in a college application are meant to derive certain specific information about the applicant. Somewhere in your profile data are the answers to any question a college asks. The first step you must take is to analyze the question. Some questions in a college application may appear

Your values and philosophy can be plugged into any question, no matter how "weird" the situation.

outlandish and strange at first, but they are aimed at discovering what you value, what life means to you, and how well you know yourself. The trick is to steer the question toward *you* and the information that you want the admissions people to know about you. If a question asks you to write about yourself in the year A.D. 2020, then your definition of happiness or success should help you. Depict yourself as a happy and successful person according to the criteria you've written about in your profile and write about *why* you are *who* you are in A.D. 2020. Your values and philosophy can be plugged into any question, no matter how "weird" the situation. Take control and look at your research material for the key to any essay question that a college may ask. The answers are all there.

Types of Essays

THERE ARE several essay patterns, or styles, that can be used to approach a question or assignment. These essay patterns can be used to design the entire essay or just specific paragraphs in the essay. Showing that you have an understanding of these styles of approach can give the admissions committee a picture of the range of your writing technique as well as add to the quality of your delivery. These various essay patterns are:

- Narrative
- Descriptive
- Definition
- Example

- Compare and contrast
- Cause and effect

How can each pattern be applied to the college application essay?

Narrative

The narrative essay tells a story. It has the voice of the storyteller and weaves a plot using a detailed, eyewitness account of events in chronological order. The tale has a beginning, a middle, and an end. A good narrative *always* assumes that the reader doesn't know anything about the story and tries to create a sense of scene and action to make the story come alive. It often explains how and why things happen in the story. And it *always* sticks to important events and avoids meaningless episodes or facts.

In your college application essay, you may find the need to tell a story or chronicle an experience. If you use this technique in a paragraph or through the entire essay, you must wear the hat of the storyteller; think of yourself as a person telling the story to an audience of strangers. You should feel a need to entertain them with important details and appeal to their senses, com-

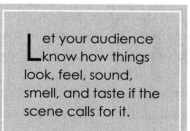

Let your audience know how things look, feel, sound, smell, and taste if the scene calls for it.

municating visually with information that is tactile and even auditory. Let your audience know how things look, feel, sound, smell, and taste if the scene calls for it. Don't just recite events. Make them live and tell the tale with a sense of time.

Some common errors that I see often in narrative essays used in the college application are as follows:

1. *Failure to describe the setting.* If you're going to tell us a story you have to describe the setting in some detail. Show us where and when the story is taking place with an attention to sensory detail that puts us "right there."

2. *Scrambling scenes.* Each paragraph in a story is determined by either place or time. If the action moves to another place (i.e., "Meanwhile, back at the ranch . . ."), you've got a new paragraph. If the time changes significantly (i.e., "Several hours later . . ."), then you've got a new paragraph.

3. *Time warps.* Make sure that when actions occur they are transitioned properly from one time to the next with time transition words (i.e., "Later . . . ," "Three hours before . . . ," "During the next month . . ."). Grammar books are loaded with transition word lists for narratives that need chronological transitions. Just think about what the audience needs in a story to get a feel for the time that's passing as the action unfolds. (See Strategy Notes at the end of this chapter.)

Descriptive

The descriptive pattern is closely related to the narrative in terms of its appeal to the senses of the audience. Pictures are all-important to the descriptive mode in your essay. If you are going to tell about a place or person, a condition, a situation, or a feeling, then you are choosing the descriptive mode. Give your subject a sensory dimension. If something is big, tell us *how big.* If you hear a sound, see a sight, or feel pain or joy, describe these things with detail or comparison. Don't just say it happened, but tell us what the experience was like for you in terms that any stranger can understand.

One note on using the descriptive mode in your essay: Don't overdo a good thing. If your language is flowery and filled with metaphor and simile, juicy with adjectives, and greased too often with adverbs, then it becomes unnatural.

Describe the events and subject matter in a voice that is real. Good storytellers "talk" their story. It should read easily and flow as if the reader were there, listening to you spin your tale. If your mouth is too full of description, the story won't read well when you tape your essay for the sound test.

Good storytellers "talk" their story.

Definition

The meaning of something that is important to you might be included in your essay. The definition mode can be used to express a sense of significance that displays your insight and grasp of an important value, virtue, belief, or concept. A definition essay usually includes the following features:

1. A personal definition. You discuss what the idea or word means in your own words.

2. A dictionary definition. You use the exact and objective definition that is traditionally known. This definition can be flat or general and needs further explanation, which makes it a good lead, forcing the reader to be interested.

3. Synonyms. You define a word by revealing other words that mean the same thing.

4. Similes and metaphors. Using these figures of speech can open up a new perspective from an unusual angle while also making your discussion of a concept such as love or truth much more visual and less heady. (You must be economical in the use of similes and metaphors.)

5. Examples. Any time you choose to discuss an idea, it's imperative to give the audience "living" examples from the real world. Examples drawn from both everyday, common experience and specific, actual events that illustrate the topic are good for bringing your ideas to the audience.

6. Comparisons. Perhaps your idea can be compared to some other idea or feeling. Tell the admissions committee what that is and illustrate the connection.

7. Negative definitions. Often the discussion of what something is *not* can serve to define it in the brightest light.

8. Anecdote. Telling a story that illustrates a concept, idea, or feeling can be the best technique for making something intangible come to life for an audience. An anecdote usually ends with a quote from one of the characters in the story that serves as a punch line to illustrate the point in a special way.

The following is a "definition essay" that embodies all the features just described. Note how the piece reveals a great deal about the person who wrote it, touching on values, beliefs, and even some scholarly research.

"Even if I had the gift of faith so that I could speak to a mountain and make it move, I would still be worth nothing at all without love." This quote from Corinthians 1:13 speaks of the importance of love. The word "love" is derived from the Latin word lubets, meaning "it pleases" (Webster's dictionary). I have been told love is very pleasing, once it is acquired.

What is love? The Webster's dictionary says that love is "A feeling of strong personal attachment induced by that which delights or commands admiration, by sympathetic understanding, or by the ties of kinship." Adoration, affection, and lust are a lot of times mistaken or accepted as love. I view love as the ultimate feeling of kindness and gentleness felt for someone or something. I see this feeling as unblemished by selfishness. Love includes a great many things: honesty, loyalty, patience, understanding. Love does not come easy; it requires a large amount of work.

Love encompasses a wide variety of good and bad ideas, concepts, and situations. Have you ever heard someone say, "Love is blind"? This statement is sometimes true. We are often kept from seeing the imperfections in our loved ones. A spouse or family of an alcoholic will often ignore the person's problem because they love the individual. However, ignoring the problem will not help the person find a solution. Thus love has closed the eyes of the lover. Another popular conception is that "love conquers all things." When two people love each other they will work out their problems no matter what it takes. "Absence makes the heart grow fonder." Few people can make a love relationship succeed when they are apart from the other. Love requires a great deal of time spent growing with the other person. To paraphrase St. Paul, without love we are powerless.

Love is like an open door. It invites you into warmth and comfort. Love is like a sled ride. The exhilaration of the ride down the hill compels you through the struggle back to the top. Love is a warming ray of sunlight on a cold and snowy day. Love does not hold grudges. It does not seek revenge. Use and abuse are not the ways of love. Love is a priceless gemstone that is to be cherished above all other emotions.

Many times I thought that I loved someone or that they loved me. Disappointment always came after a while. One day I was discussing the matter with a friend. She spoke of her disappointments with love. Then she told me of one who loved her unconditionally. No matter what happened he was always there with his arms open wide for a hug. When I asked who it was that was so perfect, she said, "My teddy bear."

Example

The example mode asks the writer to show the audience examples—typical and specific—that depict the ideas being communicated. A series of typical examples about life in the city can show readers what life is like in an urban environment. Just saying that the city is a weird world is not nearly as powerful as showing typical city weirdness. Adding a specific example, in the form of an anecdote, brings you into the story and keeps the focus on you. A series of brief anecdotes to illustrate your idea or feeling will be strong statements about how you relate to what you believe or feel. It's showtime, so use examples that paint a clear picture of what you mean.

Compare and Contrast

The compare-and-contrast (C & C) mode in your essay can fit your purpose if you want to express a before-and-after experience. If you choose this method, there are two approaches you can use. One is the block method and the other is the point-by-point style of C & C.

The block method utilizes two paragraphs. The first paragraph describes, for example, the "before" you, and the second paragraph describes the "after" you. In the point-by-point method, you must use one paragraph; you merely move from one "before" example in a sentence to an "after" example in the next sentence, and then continue to repeat this process throughout the paragraph. Of course, the before-and-after illustration is only one of many topics that can use the C & C mode. You can use this writing pattern to communicate any kind of changed relationship in your experience.

Cause and Effect

An old Latin proverb states that "times change and we change with them." The cause-and-effect mode is about change. It is a writing pattern concerned with how things change and why they change, the causes of change, and the effects that change has on people, places, and things. It is ideal for illustrating your awareness of what is happening around you and to you. If you decide to take a direction in your essay that will concentrate on your growth in some area or time in your life, then the cause-and-effect paragraph form or essay pattern can be a valuable technique.

The approach in this format offers you three alternatives: (1) You can zero in on causes that have influenced you; (2) you can focus on the effects of one particular force in your life; or

(3) you can discuss both the causes and effects of change in your life during a particular time. The "cause" portion demands merely that you state in your topic sentence words to the effect that something caused certain important things to occur; then detail how that something influenced the change. The "effect" portion is concerned with what happened because of that change. It describes the changes that resulted from this influential event, discovery, or person. Both parts demand a detailed description of either *how* or *what*. You should also discuss why the "cause" was influential and why the changes occurred. This can add dimension to your college application essay.

Suppose that you discuss the influence that a person has had on your life. If you merely discuss the person and not why you were influenced by the individual, then you take yourself out of the essay, and that is a major mistake. Perhaps you wish to discuss the different ways that you changed due to a specific event. To mention only the changes and neglect to speak to the reasons why the changes occurred can also be a mistake.

Use the cause-and-effect mode if you decide to write about a change or growth

> Use the cause-and-effect mode if you decide to write about a change or growth event in your life.

event in your life. Describe the force that made the change happen, outlining why it was such an important factor in moving you to a different place in your heart or head. Then talk about the ways you changed because of the force or event, telling why the changes took place. Remember the three questions that must be answered in the cause-and-effect mode: *how, what happened,* and *why* (which must be applied to explain both the causes and the effects).

Any or all of these essay patterns can be used in your college application essay paragraphs. If you use a brief anecdote to illustrate a facet of your character, then you are in the narrative mode. If you decide to discuss a virtue or value that is significant to you, such as courage or determination, you use the definition mode. You use the example mode to illustrate an idea such as success or happiness. You can use either the compare-and-contrast mode or the cause- and-effect mode to address a personal growth issue. These patterns can be applied directly, paragraph by paragraph, to your college application essay. You don't have to be stuck at 3 A.M. on the night before the mailing deadline with no clue about how to approach your topics. You have these techniques to use. It is possible to write a great essay using the narrative mode in the first paragraph, the definition mode in the second paragraph, the compare-and-contrast mode in the third paragraph, the cause-and-effect mode in the fourth paragraph, and the descriptive mode in the last paragraph. Variety can keep a reader's attention far more effectively than any one style. Variety also suggests that you know how to write in more than one way. Use the patterns that best suit your content.

> Well-written paragraphs answer questions before they are asked.

Strategy Notes

Answer the Questions. In your rough draft, underline the clearly presented topic sentences in each paragraph. Next, look at each topic sentence and write down, on a separate sheet of paper, questions you think a stranger might ask about the topic or the focus of the topic sentence (i.e., *who* questions; *what* questions; *where, when, why,* and *how* questions—as many as you can think of). Be detached and objective while you're writing the questions. Now, read the rest of your paragraph. Did you answer these questions with enough detail to satisfy the curiosity of a reader? Well-written paragraphs answer questions before they are asked.

Detail, Example, and Explanation Series. This is a good method for supporting a topic sentence in a paragraph. First, write a detailed sentence that clarifies the topic with concrete details and information. Then, follow up with a sentence that uses an example to clarify the topic. Lastly, provide an explanation of the topic sentence. You can repeat this series more than once in a paragraph, especially if there is a variety of angles on the topic that you would like to discuss. Try this out by writing a paragraph on any one of the profile subjects in chapter 3 and see if it works for you.

Time, Space, and Importance. Transition words, which link sentences together logically, are the keys to writing any effective paragraph and are often the difference between excellent and poor writing. Words such as *later, afterwards,* and *subsequently,* for example, are used for time transitions. There are similar terms that link sentences that describe spatial relationships (e.g., *next to, near, beneath*) and the order of importance (e.g., *first, secondly, lastly*). (Your high school grammar text should have a complete list of transition words for time, space, and importance.) These terms, and the many others like them, are often missing in college application essays, which makes the work choppy and amateurish.

You and I. The use of the second person *you* in the college application essay should always be avoided because it is considered colloquial and very poor writing technique. Unless the essay prompt is asking you to demonstrate some activity (e.g., "Tell us the correct way to eat an ice cream cone"), you should not use the second person except in quoted dialogue.

You should also be careful about redundancy of the first person at the beginning of every sentence. Of course it's tough to avoid using *I* when you're writing about yourself, but if you show us more than tell us about your experiences, it will lessen the "I did this . . . I did that . . . blah, blah, blah." Create images and actual events and describe them with concrete, sensory detail, and you'll find that the first person will be less prominent and repetitive in your essay.

7

The Good, the Bad, and the Ugly

Sample Essays

We learn through example. Reading successful college application essays can be a useful tool for revealing the kinds of approaches and elements that should be present in your essay. Sample essays let you know what the standards are and what is allowed. Your guidance counselor may have a file of essays written by graduates from your high school that were outstanding in some way. You might ask to see some of these essays if you think this will help you get ideas. You must realize, however, that someone else's great essay is not going to be a blueprint for *your* great essay. Your style and content will be different. Your life and experiences are different from everyone else's; therefore you don't want to get caught in the trap of trying to model your essay after the work of someone who isn't you.

The following essays are presented as examples of certain qualities that you should consider as you write your unique essay. Of these five essays, three are very good and two are . . .

well, not so good. After each essay are comments that discuss the important points illustrated by these essays. Perhaps the most valuable essays for you will be the "not-so-good" submissions, because they exhibit the things you should avoid and that are common to application essays failing to reveal positive images of the college candidate.

ESSAY ONE

After having the temperature of my pupils taken and enduring what seemed gallons of eyedrop fluid, I was asked to read the eye chart while the nurse determined my fate based on my answers. One of the first difficulties was trying to find the eye chart on the white-plastered wall. Squinting, I located it and began my test. I would cry confidently, "D," and glance over to see any form of suggestion on the nurse's face, but nothing was there except cool efficiency.

A fairly common problem that faces people today is the inability to read the indicated line on the eye chart. At the age of thirteen I was taken to my optometrist for my first encounter with the eye chart because I could no longer see the blackboard at my all-girl Catholic school, and was also suffering from constant headaches. I had always assumed that the world beyond ten feet was fuzzy and that everyone saw it the same way. This misconception was clarified the day I had my brown, marble-shaded eyes examined and was told I was nearsighted. At the end of my Ordeal with the Eye Chart I came out of the optometrist's office, not with a smile on my face, but rather, a frame on my nose. I was myopic and became one of the many people destined to wear glasses and keep Ray Ban in a thriving business. Wearing glasses not only changed the way I saw life, but it offered a difference that I live with daily and from which I learn to prosper.

When I received my first pair of corrective lenses, I could see things that I had once missed. Road signs were no longer a blotch of blurry color, but rather, definite symbols of meaning. I no longer had to sit in the front row of a movie theatre to enjoy a film. I could also participate in one of my favorite sports, basketball. My brown-rimmed spectacles seemed to hug my ears quite comfortably while I ran for a lay-up. I found myself able to assist my parents when trying to read the screen of departing flights at the airport before we left on our next family vacation. When taking my driver's test I started out on the right foot by being able to locate and recite the eye chart with ease. I could now see what enabled me to pass my driver's test, which brought me responsibilities along with a new car. I would no longer shy away from activities that required perfect eyesight, but on the other hand, I would reach in my purse and pull out my passport to vision— my glasses. I was at one point in the early stage of my "new sight" embarrassed to wear my glasses, afraid of what people might think, but then I realized I was not about to sacrifice my vision for a few moments of false image. Instead people would have to accept and like me for my imperfect self or just have to stop seeing themselves in the reflection of my plastic lenses.

Friends usually have mixed feelings about drastic changes in the ones they love. Sure enough, mine had a sundry of comments about the "new me." In the eyes of some of my cronies I am viewed as a secretary or businesswoman look-alike. There are always those classmates who ask to look through my glasses and I hand them over with trepidation. When my delicate lenses are passed among several friends who try them on, they take them off suddenly because everything is magnified to terrifying proportions. Inevitably my spectacles are returned with dozens of fingerprints imprinted on both lenses and the predictable comment, "How can you see through these? You must be blind." When this occurs it reminds me of how differently everyone views the world. Some view it clearly and easily while others need the help of something or someone to keep things in perspective. No decision is arrived upon without some outside input; therefore people should keep others' points of view in mind when deciding upon anything of importance.

Glasses have their disadvantages and at some points can be a nuisance. In Chemistry, for example, I had to wear my glasses under the required goggles, which could get quite uncomfortable and painful, crushing the bridge of my nose between two incompatible frames with every movement of my head. Spectacles are unforgiving companions because should I forget them at home it is impossible to have a good time without them. All, however, are fascinated at how the combination of sweat and gravity can make my glasses slip down my nose and over my upper lip. Nearsightedness does have its advantages. Those who are myopic must take more time to scrutinize the little details that make life worthwhile, and develop a virtue known to few as "Patience." Those of us who see the world through corrective lenses tend not to be easily distracted and can be trusted and relied upon for our focus.

My life in the world of myopia has taught me that everyone sees the world differently and that a difference of perspectives affects the way people make their decisions about everything. One cannot judge a person just because they are extremely different in style or appearance or even because their differences are slight and few. On the other hand everyone should be allowed to express their views of the world with freedom. The cliche goes, "You can never really know a person until you have walked a mile in their shoes." In my case I believe that you can never really appreciate someone's perspective until you have seen the horizon through their crafted lenses.

The essay is rich in detail and insight, as well as containing some self-deprecating humor.

This essay is a vivid example of how little things can mean a great deal. The writer reveals her personality and perspective, using images of real events and what they mean to her. The experience of wearing glasses is common enough. Many people wear corrective lenses. This writer takes that simple experience, makes it live for us, and shows the readers that there is something that can be learned from myopia. The essay is rich in detail and insight, as well as containing some self-deprecating humor. Each paragraph has a topic sentence and a well-developed purpose. The essay is positive and concerns itself with learning and understanding. The leads in each paragraph entice us to read on, and the clinchers finish each paragraph with reflective thought. Though the essay runs longer than is usually advisable, it still holds our attention to the very end.

ESSAY TWO

Redwood Trees. Their scarred bark spells silent stories of time passed, of strange and wondrous survival. Filtered light falls, allowing the webs of surrounding ferns to glow. No breeze upsets the delicate green knitting. Soft air suspends a canopy of innumerable needles. Sound is delicate.

I've sat at the foot of one of these mute grandparents many times, pressing my back into its strength, savoring its stillness.

The first chance I had to experience the redwoods was through my freshman biology class. Each spring the biology teachers at my school organize a week-long trip to the coast. Campus becomes busy and anticipation runs high. Tents are set up all over the lawns, more sagging than standing. Students string sample lines into a "tidepool" on the hockey field and catalogue paper "crustaceans." Bio students call non-bio students "foraminifera heads," then laugh.

However, nothing is ample preparation for the real thing. Trees which were merely large on videotape become massive and awe-inspiring when actually touched. To we who live in the high desert, surrounded by dust and sagebrush, the spectacle of lush, layered walls of ferns is breathtaking. Even slimy banana slugs take on a mystical appearance.

The intense feelings the redwoods give me will remain forever. Sharing the moment a friend first saw the ocean . . . Crouching to the side of a trail, sketching wildflowers . . . Watching the sun set from a jutting rock being boomed by waves far below. These were the most important, most truly educational experiences of the last four years.

This essay was written in response to a question that asked the student to "Describe the educational experience—formal or informal—that has had the most significant impact on your life." The response is short and sweet. Detail and reflection abound in this piece. It paints a picture of the experience and tells us what the event meant to the student in images and thoughts. The essay doesn't have to be a full 500 words if the feelings and personal perspectives can be told in fewer words with honest, straightforward language. The writer controls this essay by using show and tell to its best advantage. His entire life can't be captured in this essay, but the appreciation he has for these important moments is clearly reflected in the details and impressions expressed in the piece. When the essay question asks you to *describe* an experience, then you must use detail and insight to make the essay work to your advantage. "Oooohs" and "aaaahs" are not enough. *Show* the experience, as did this writer, and then *tell* what it means to you.

> The writer controls this essay by using show and tell to its best advantage.

ESSAY THREE

On a sunny day in 1982, I borded a plane to begin my trip around the world. I felt both excited and scared not knowing exactly what lay ahead. I embarked upon eleven foreign lands which included: Hong Kong, China, Japan, Indonesia, Thailand, India, the Seyshelles Islands, Kenya, France, and England. Although each country had its own personality, Kenya touched me in a special way. What I saw and felt on the first day the jeep headed out on the Masai Mara was more fulfilling than my highest expectations.

The sun rose quietly out of the tall grass on the savanna waking all forms of life to greet its warmth. The sky's hue changed to royal blue and white clouds floated easily in the heavens. Along the horizon, a herd of elephants swayed through the grass. As we came closer, I discovered baby elephants trailing like a caboose behind their mothers. Every elephant walked in the same direction as if a destination was awaiting them. Suddenly, my heart rose for just beyond the jeep a pride of lions lounged in the shade of a tree. The male lion looked like a great king, wearing his royal headdress, while watching his heirs tumble in the grass. In the distance, appeared hundreds of prancing gazelles. Immediately, three of the lions dashed away to capture their prey. Preceding their departure, a vulture flew overhead as a sign to us that the prey had been caught. The scene created mixed emotions for me. On one hand the killing made me angry, yet on the other hand, I knew it was necessary for the lions' survival. From observing the wildlife on the Masai Mara, I realized that the lives of the animals were only a simplified version of our life as humans. Everyday we fight to survive. Basically, our motivation for success is our desire to survive physically and mentally. We create organizations, such as governments, to supply order in our communities. We depend on family and friends to give us love and support. Most of all we need food, clothing, and shelter in order to live. Our life may have more complications, but at the core humans and animals are both motivated by their desire to survive. The idea of all these animals as a metaphor for my life made the gap between us closer. For once, I was in the cage and the animals were free. I saw myself in the animals. I identified with the pride of the lion, the exuberance of the gazelle, and the peace of the elephant. I discovered the qualities we both share. I felt at one with, not only the animals, but the universe.

The colors of the land and sky were fading with the dying sun as the jeep headed for camp. The cool air blew through my hair as I watched the day come to an end. In the twilight, I closed my eyes and imagined the day to come.

From the outset, this essay has problems. A word is misspelled in the opening sentence—a disastrous mistake. Punctuation errors are evident throughout the writing—an equally perilous red flag. The second paragraph runs on endlessly and is filled

> This essay should have focused more on what the experiences meant and not so incessantly on what was seen.

with flowery descriptions of very typical jungle scenes that don't do anything for the candidate. There is obviously a downside to detail. If you describe an event and leave yourself out of it, then the essay isn't about you, it's about the event. A car advertisement may talk about the road for a few seconds, but it will spend far more time discussing how the car handles the road. In this piece we read a litany of clichés about the experience, with very little reflection on each image. This essay should have focused more on what the experiences meant and not so incessantly on what was seen. The final note that should be considered in this essay is that it rambles into oblivion, touching on points of concern for the student in the final sentences but never developing them. The college application essay can be an opportunity to tell the admissions committee what you think about a certain few issues, but not about dozens of issues and ideas. Perhaps the most important lesson to be learned from this essay is that it was written at the last minute, had no objective eye to proof it, and didn't have a clear plan.

ESSAY FOUR

You might have surmised, after glancing at my hostile cumulative record and SAT scores, that my scholastic inclinations have reflected nothing but sheer mediocrity. I've always held marginal tendencies towards anything educational. Oh, I love learning, mind you, I savor any experience, good or bad, like it was a piece of butterscotch candy. I invest it in my memory, in hopes that it will flourish and become essential to me later in life. But true education, the education found only through experience and devastation, is the education that eventually evolves into wisdom. And it is wisdom I am seeking, not an impressive grade point average. I'm sorry to disappoint you. I just condemn this tedious process of being evaluated, educationally distilled, spiritually dissected, and intellectually abused. It would seem only logical that I should be evaluated on how many continents I've been to (four) and on how many nations I've visited (twenty-one) and on the various cultures I've beheld. I should be tested on how many countries I've lived in during my early youth (three) and how many different schools I was forced to adjust to before graduating from high school (nine). I should most definitely be graded on how well I was recently able to ascend from my abysmal realm of manic depression. The degree of my misery was so horribly severe and overwhelming, I can see how none of you staunch, caustic admissions officers could comprehend such a discrepancy in a prospective college student. But I felt you should know. I wouldn't want to beguile you into believing I was perfect, which is probably what most students claim to be in THEIR college essays. I believe my transcript neglected to mention that I tutor illiterate people, and that my idol is a twenty-eight year old homeless man in Reseda, by the name of Beatle John, who writes poetry. Or that I write poetry. Or that my reading interests include Dostoyevsky and books on Zen Buddhism. Did you know that I was transitorily in love with Ivan, the intellectual atheist, in *The Brothers Karamazov,* and identify myself immensely with Alceste in *Misanthrope*? Surely not. My transcript fails to mention any of that. It's bureaucracy, if you ask me. Absolutely animal. I'm sincerely sorry I offended you like this, but I'll sacrifice my acceptance into your noble institution for an opportunity to be liberated in expressing my true feelings concerning education. I think, in thirty of forty years, I'll be able to say I acquired the most education in high school. But that it wasn't in the classroom.

Please excuse this one-paragraph literary mess of animosity and delirium. Thank you for allowing me to be true and honest, and I sincerely hope my transcript seems a bit less significant in its importance after this "essay."

This essay is a tragedy. It is obviously written by someone who is intelligent but does not know what he or she is doing. It is negative, paranoid, and confrontational, and it rambles incessantly. It begins by declaring that the student is a "loser." It flaunts a low grade point average as a sign of success and tries to portray a rebellious, misunderstood teen who really "has it together" far more than the "numbers" indicate. When I first read this essay, I cringed. It was self-destructive and badly advised. Obviously, this student has a problem with being judged and takes out the frustration in the essay. The college application essay is not a place to plead your case for different evaluation techniques in the world of education. Being so presumptuous as to assume what other students may be writing and accusing the admissions officers of being "staunch and caustic" shows remarkably poor judgment. This indicates that the student may have the vocabulary to read a college textbook but is lacking the maturity to survive the freshman year of classes. If you write an essay that is anything like this, your cause is doomed.

> This essay is a tragedy. If you write an essay that is anything like this, your cause is doomed.

ESSAY FIVE

The five of us huddled inside the tiny tent—brother, father, son, uncle, cousin. Even by four in the morning, the pouring rain had not stopped its eight-hour marathon shower, and the confines of the ridiculously small three-person tent had not gotten any larger. Frigid water soaked my legs, and I tried in vain to identify the owner of the elbow jutting into my back, preventing me from sleeping. Outside, the fury of the storm's lightning and hailstones mocked our insignificant tent, leaving us at the mercy of Nature. Many times I nearly succumbed to the temptation to hike out and seek shelter in a dry car, but I could not face the numbing rain outside. So, in the wee hours of the gray morning, I emerged with a look that would evoke pity in the hardest of hearts—numb, aching and worn, I was ready to go home.

It seems to be an immutable law of nature that fishing trips never go just right, sometimes much less right than expected. But I always enjoy them because they allow me a few precious hours away from my life in the busy city. I have learned to value the time I spend up in the wilderness of the Sierra Nevada as a time of rejuvenation, a time to remember just what life's all about: respect, education and family.

Fly-fishing is nothing if not an act of homage to fish everywhere. As my Uncle Jerome has always told me, "Christopher, the fish is smarter than you think. If you can see him, he can see you." Fishing is an act of deception that cannot be taken lightly. If the fish spots me, doesn't buy my rendition of a Caddis fly, or detects a fake-looking drag on my line, I walk away empty-handed. But on the occasions when I am lucky enough, crouching in the damp grass beside a small stream to land a golden trout, an *Oncorhynchus mykiss aguabonita,* and to hold it in my hands, I am faced with a rainbow of colors that a box of Crayolas could not hope to create. The delicate yellow of its belly blends with bright oranges and reds into a blue-gray body that is more smooth than a river-washed stone. Scientists have said that to know life is to love it; I believe that to *fish* is to love Nature.

The experience of fishing evokes more than respect; it is truly an act of learning. Some things a biology text cannot teach adequately. Should we protect nature? I intend to spend my life trying to. But why? Certainly not because a concerned biologist says I ought to. I remember hiking several grueling miles near Mt. Whitney and suddenly finding myself in the middle of the most beautiful meadow I had ever seen. Through this gem in the wilderness flowed Cottonwood Creek, bordered by soft grasses and round rocks. All around sprouted the pinks of the Sierra primrose and the purples of the Jeffrey shooting star, and behind the trees rose Mt. Langley, a towering peak of granite. This is why I respect Nature; this is why I want to protect it. To fish there, in the most beautiful place on Earth, taught me the importance of preserving what I love.

But fishing has never been meaningful for me without the presence of my family. Never have I trekked out to the mountains lacking my father or uncle or cousin. It's almost paradoxical: the act of fishing is such a solitary business, but the celebration of a catch is truly a celebration among friends. Even on that prolonged night, wet and cold and hurting, I would rather have had all five of us in that cramped tent than to have been comfortable. For together we could laugh at our predicament and share the moment, doing what we love in the best place in the world to do it. That's what life is all about.

If there ever was an essay that captures the essence of show and tell in a college application personal statement, this is it. I had the pleasure of watching this essay grow from draft to draft, and the writer literally crafted this piece with a painter's touch, starting from a rough sketch to a fleshed-out drawing, and then adding fine touches of detail, color, and nuance of phrasing to achieve the final canvas. The essay does several things very well. It tells a story in anecdote form, the "cramped-tent" episode taking us immediately to the scene of the essay with a detailed action sequence, filled with intelligence, sensitivity to detail, and graphic use of visual and tactile imagery. Proof that it's the little things that count is clearly offered here. As well, the first paragraph leaves us with a sentence ("I was ready to go home.") that allows the anecdote to function like a blind lead that moves into the paragraphs that follow, building interest. Of course, the rest of the piece has great effect because of its further use of superb technique, such as Uncle Jerome's quote on the fish—it's always important to have someone say something in dialogue in the essay, and the more personally connected to you they are the better. (See Somebody Say Something! in chapter 5) The use of specialized details such as the biological term for the fish, and the exact names for the flowers and the mountains and creek—these subtle touches say very clearly to the admissions committee that this student pays intelligent, careful attention to detail, without being pompous or trivial. The writer knows the universe around him or her at more than a superficial level and cares about the uniqueness of place and time. The final element of style that the essay reveals is a keen sense of definition. This essay is packed with meaning—emotional, technical, and intellectual. The writer is self-deprecating, defining what he learns from simple experiences, re-creating images that *show* us the learning in real-life detail, not telling us the "meaning of life" but rather, showing us "what life is all about." (See Definition Essays in chapter 6.)

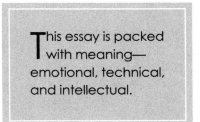

This essay is packed with meaning—emotional, technical, and intellectual.

In the final analysis, any essay that uses the techniques and honest revelation of personal experience that we see in this simple examination of a family fishing tradition will be a success.

8

Under Pressure:
The *SAT II: Writing Test*

Have you been asked to take the *SAT II: Writing Test* as part of your application process for any of your college choices? Chances are that more and more students will begin to see this writing examination as part of their junior and senior year battery of tests for college admission. There are several reasons for this circumstance. Recently, I spoke to the College Board people about the SAT II because the new SAT written essay is a subject of great interest to my students in courses and workshops. The new exams have become a major event and will impact students significantly in various ways, and the College Board has continued to be very helpful in answering my questions about the written portion of the exam.

Actually, not everyone who takes the SAT will have to take the writing test. This will be a part of your application only if you are required by "Lucky U." to take it as an "achievement test." However, one of the reasons that the new writing test was changed and is being marketed by CEEB (The College Entrance Examination Board) is because many colleges asked for a writing test that they could trust, because they were skeptical about the legitimacy of many of the application essays that they read in their applications. Before the test was ever introduced, more than 180 colleges asked to use it as part of their admissions testing package. That number continues to grow, in my estimation, because writing ability is the yardstick by which successful, liberal-arts college students are judged. The test becomes a kind of validation for your college essays, or a red flag that warns admissions people to beware of a stellar essay in the application that is written by a student who scored a 2 or 1 on the *SAT II: Writing Test.* The test is also a clear indicator to colleges of your ability to write a formal, standardized essay that can "make the grade" in a competitive college atmosphere. What does all this mean? In a few words, it means you better know a few things about writing "under pressure," because the SAT II is a twenty-minute writing test.

> # W riting ability is the yardstick by which successful, liberal-arts college students are judged.

Twenty Minutes!!!

The *SAT II: Writing Test* is designed to determine how well you write. The time allotted for this sample of your writing skills is exactly twenty minutes. The idea of writing something "brilliant" in twenty minutes might sound scary, especially when your best friend is a math whiz and says, "That's only 1200 seconds!" Should you scream in anguish and allow yourself to be overcome with eye-bulging, heart-stopping rigor mortis at

BASIC INFORMATION ABOUT THE *SAT II: WRITING TEST*

Here is some basic information about the *SAT II: Writing Test*.

- *Type of test:* Impromptu essay test

- *Length of test:* Twenty minutes

- *Topic:* Always the defense of a personal perspective on a particular philosophical issue or "truth"

- *Length of essay:* One paragraph minimum. Three paragraph essays are a preferable length

- *Judges:* Writing teachers and professors from across the United States (usually English teachers). Two readers per student test

- *Grading technique:* Holistic

- *Grade scale:* 1 to 6 (lowest to highest possible) or 200 points. Each numeric score equals 30 points. Two scorers per test with scores combined (i.e., a 4 and a 6 would add up to a total of 10. Multiply that total by 15 and your score is 150, plus 20 points for your name, equaling 170.)

the thought of all this pressure? *No.* This time limit is not all that scary if you know what the people who are scoring the test are looking for when they read the essays.

Cut to the Chase

ELABORATING ON the information contained in the above sidebar, we'll discuss each element of the test as it appears on the list.

Impromptu

The test is impromptu, and this means you won't have any extra time to prepare for it other than what you use in the twenty-minute total time allowed. The beauty of an "impromptu essay" is that it will reveal all of your immediate and ready skills. Bringing in a memorized essay won't work, because any essay that strays from the topic or refuses to deal with the topic directly will receive an automatic lowest possible score, regardless of how perfect the prose. The "up side" of an impromptu essay is that the graders are instructed by the chief scorer to treat the essays as first drafts and therefore to "go easy" on *occasional* errors in punctuation or syntax. Even papers without a final conclusion are to be treated kindly, due to the impromptu nature of the test.

Time Allowed

Don't start writing your essay the instant after you have finished reading the topic and instructions. Stop and think for a few seconds. The amount of verbiage means nothing in this test. This test is about *quality.* The road to quality is paved with forethought and planning; if you panic and start writing immediately, there's a good chance that your essay will start with a weak opening paragraph, and that is death in this kind of test. Take a few minutes to sort out what you think about the essay topic. Take a look at the way the topic is stated. Look for key words that will tell you what writing techniques the essay is asking you to utilize in the presentation of your ideas. Are they asking you to *define* something? Is the question asking you to provide an *example* to support your ideas? Is an *expla-*

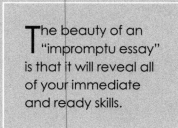

The beauty of an "impromptu essay" is that it will reveal all of your immediate and ready skills.

nation of your position being requested? You better decide on the course or direction you will take toward the topic *before* you write a sentence of the essay. *Plan ahead.* If you spend the first three to five minutes planning your structure, you will have a solid fifteen minutes at the very least to execute an essay that at the bottom line will say, "A calm, thoughtful person wrote this."

Topics

Below, you will find a recent example of the kind of "prompt" or essay topic that was used in a recent SAT writing exam.

Consider carefully the following quotation and the assignment below it. Then plan and write your essay as directed.

> "Any advance involves some loss."

Assignment: *Choose a specific example from personal experience, current events, or from your reading in history, literature, or other subjects and use this example as a basis for an essay in which you agree or disagree with the statement above. Be sure to be specific.*

This is a typical essay topic on the *SAT II: Writing Test.* The use of a quote, and one that usually states a philosophical position that begs for elaboration on the part of the writer, has appeared on at least 14 out of the last 17 SAT writing tests given as achievement exams since 1983. I think we can declare a trend here. In nearly every prompt used in these tests, students were asked to agree or disagree with the statement given, and then to provide a defense of their perspective by use of examples from history, current affairs, literature, or personal experience.

Though your ability to allude to literary and historical subjects in the essay may be useful in supporting your position on the topic, it is not necessary to wear the academic hat when you write your response. One of the guidelines given to those teachers who will grade the tests is a caution about literary and historical allusions in the essays. Graders are told to avoid awarding points to a paper merely because the essay mentions literary or historical examples. As well, teachers at the grading table are also directed to never downgrade a paper that does not use academic examples. It comes down to this: How well did you write about the topic? Your ability to quote Keats or Somerset Maugham, or the fact that the Crimean Wars or Mary Stuart are included in your treatment of the topic, will not have nearly as much influence on your final score as your ability to communicate clearly and with a structure that reveals your understanding of the rules of written argument, that is, the expository essay.

Is your own life experience good enough to use as supportive example in the essay? Absolutely. Again, it's how well you frame your response to the essay question that counts. Read the question carefully. The previous sample question tells the writer exactly what kind of essay is needed. The Example Essay is the primary rhetorical mode for this question, as is clearly directed in the assignment. If the essay that you write uses a standard expository essay approach and practices the following general techniques, the test prompt can be covered in three solid paragraphs, and in fifteen minutes.

PARAGRAPH ONE (The first of two options): A Thesis Paragraph. Begin the paragraph with a solid lead. The sentence can be either a freak lead (see page 126) or a standard lead that comes in the form of a strong declarative sentence. The goal is to get to a clear topic within two sentences. Don't restate the prompt verbatim in this paragraph but, instead, rephrase the prompt in your own words and create your topic sentence from that paraphrase. Avoid the immediately personal approach that begins with, "I agree with the statement, . . . blah, blah, etc." State a position and don't personalize the essay unless you use an example that happens to be a personal anecdote. Define the quote in your own words, or paraphrase it, so that it becomes *your* thought, without saying, "I think . . . etc." It is very important to try to avoid first-person commentary in a test of this kind, except when relating a personal account that supports the thesis of the essay. Otherwise, the writing comes off as amateurish and unpolished. Use of a typical example that supports the first paragraph's thesis is also a good technique that can be used in this opening paragraph. End the paragraph with a solid, reflective clincher. (See chapter 6, "It's Showtime!")

(The second option): A Narrative Paragraph. Instead of beginning your essay with a thesis paragraph, you may begin with an anecdote that clearly illustrates your position. This technique can get the reader immediately into your essay and is a refreshing beginning. Of course, this means that you must follow up in paragraph two with a declarative sentence that states the position of the essay, and proceed to outline the reasons and explanations for your argument.

PARAGRAPH TWO: Descriptive/Narrative Paragraph. Remember that the Law of Show and Tell is absolutely fundamental in this essay test, as it is in all good expository essay writing. Always support every concept with an illustration or detail that quickly follows it, and always follow an illustration with a concept that further explains something about

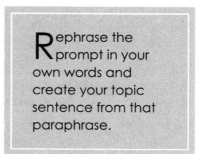

Rephrase the prompt in your own words and create your topic sentence from that paraphrase.

that illustration. "Show and Tell" or "Tell and Show" are inseparable in effective writing. If you begin your essay in paragraph one with a thesis paragraph, using explanatory prose that tells the reader what your position on the topic is, be sure to use paragraph two for your examples in support of the thesis. Use a narrative mode if you can in paragraph two, because it demonstrates your ability to move from one style to another with some ease and demonstrates your ability to use an extended example, as is often required in the essay test. The narrative also takes the essay out of the conceptual mode and brings it into the visual mode. The key here is to set up the narrative with a good lead that frames the paragraph with a connection to the topic and to finish paragraph two with a clincher sentence that reaffirms the "story" as evidence that supports your particular philosophical position.

PARAGRAPH THREE: The Ethos Paragraph. If you have time for more than three paragraphs after planning your essay for a few minutes, that will be a luxury. Let's assume you're writing a three-paragraph essay and that your final paragraph is your closing paragraph. This paragraph is much like a lawyer's summation to a jury at the end of a trial in court. Ethos is a Greek term that means the moral nature or guiding belief. The final paragraph expresses the ethos of the essay, just as a good lawyer expresses the ethos or guiding belief of his or her case during final summation. It is not a restatement of the first paragraph, however. It should take the tone of an enlightened overview of the topic, and it is also the one place in the essay where you may express your opinion, based on the evidence that you have previously introduced. Like an attorney, your summation should not introduce conclusions that your preceding paragraphs cannot support. You may, within reason, extrapolate on the possible significance of your conclusions, however. The jury (and the readers of the essay test) don't want to be confused with an entirely new argument at the end of the essay. They merely want you to tie all the evidence and your original opening argument together. If you reflect in a thoughtful manner on the significance of your philosophical position at the end of your essay, then you will have done the job. If you ramble all over the topic, change direction, and lose focus on the plan you outlined in the first five minutes, then your client may also lose the case . . . and you know who the client is.

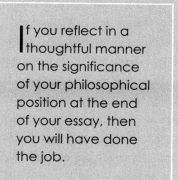

If you reflect in a thoughtful manner on the significance of your philosophical position at the end of your essay, then you will have done the job.

Sample topics from the exam will follow at the end of this chapter, but first take a look at the sample quotation mentioned previously ("Any advance . . ."). Put a clock in front of you and give yourself twenty minutes to write the essay. (I am assuming at this point that you have already read the chapter in this book entitled "It's Showtime!" You know, then, how important good paragraph structure is, the value of good leads and clinchers, and the importance of transitions between sentences in a paragraph. If you haven't read the chapter, please do so now.) All right, then. Back to the clock. Write clearly and legibly. *Go!*

Judges, Grading Technique, and Scores

IN 1991, during a five-day stretch in December, 181 high school and college English teachers met to grade 80,000 writing tests like the one you may be taking. Even my rather elusive math skills tell me that each teacher corrected an average of 888 tests in that week. Ouch! Oh, you think I'm way off in my calculations? Surprisingly, I'm exactly right. In the SAT writing test, each test is corrected by *two teachers*. I'm sure that means that some of these graders are reading nearly two hundred essays a day. How do they do that?

During the nine years since '91 the technique for judging the essays has not changed. The technique used to score the tests is called "Holistic Scoring." It's the same scoring strategy used to score the writing segment of Advanced Placement examinations (A.P. exams). This is basically how it works. Each essay is read very quickly, and graders are told to read for an impression of the entire paper. (That's why structure is so important to you when you write it.) Scorers are not allowed to reread or analyze the paper. It's a one shot deal, and teachers start making up their minds about the score of the test immediately. I've done it with A.P. exams, and it's the closest thing to Zen grading I have ever seen. Scorers are given a list of 16 guidelines. These instructions create a uniformity of judgment on the quality of writing for every paper, or at least the hope is to do so. Graders are told to read "supportively," that is, to reward students for what they do well, rather than to penalize students for what they omit or do badly. They are told to ignore the length of the paper as a criterion for a good grade. Short papers may often be very good and long papers are sometimes "atrocious" (their word, not mine). An unfinished but developed paper is not penalized for lacking a conclusion. Use of literary or historical examples doesn't make a paper inherently better than one that uses a personal example to defend a point. Graders are told to ignore handwriting. If they can't read what you wrote, the paper is given to a table leader who has the unenviable job of attempting to decipher a cryptic script. The readers are told to remember that the writers are seventeen and eighteen years old and not middle-aged philosophers. In other words, you're not marked down for an occasionally naive or idealistic perspective. As well, the scorers are told to remember that students had only twenty minutes to write the essays. It's *how* you write that counts. Does spelling count? Diction? Sentence structure? Yes. Everything counts . . . as a whole.

The scores are from 1 to 6, with 6 being best. Graders are asked on the first day to read "range finders" before they begin reading and scoring exam papers. These essay samples give the graders a sense of what is representative of each of the six score levels. These samples were already scored by the chief readers and table leaders and are used as models for the next 80,000 papers or more that will be read. There is no "average score" in this test. Either a paper is above average (6, 5, and 4) or below average (3, 2, and 1). Readers are told not to be afraid of awarding papers a 6 or a 5, because each paper is judged against the others. There is no "heavenly scale" in this test (that is, a perfect 6 that can only be achieved by The Supreme Word Wiz).

> Clarity is always the ultimate goal in any essay, and the best way to achieve it is to write in a voice that is natural and accessible.

During the course of the test scoring, each of the readers is monitored by a table leader and the other chief scorers to ensure that Mr. Jones or Ms. Grundy isn't awarding 6s or 1s to essays that should be receiving different scores. In fact, the people who score these tests are very accomplished and fair teachers. They are looking for a demonstration of good writing technique. An above-average essay is highly achievable for you if you follow the above guidelines and practice on the topics that appear below.

As you read and practice on the essays that follow, try to concentrate on "teaching" the reader about your particular point of view. Assume nothing. Help the reader learn about what you think, using all the means at your disposal, such as examples, details, descriptions, anecdotes, and definitions. Don't try to write in an intellectual tone. Clarity is always the ultimate goal in any essay, and the best way to achieve it is to write in a voice that is natural and accessible. Just as you should write from the heart in your personal statement in the college application, your SAT essay test should use a voice that speaks from the heart.

Sample Essay Topics

1. *"People are introduced to themselves by their misfortunes."* To what extent do you agree or disagree with this statement? Discuss, using specific examples from history, current affairs, literature, or personal observation to support your conclusions.

2. *"Few of the men and women of today who have attained hero status exemplify enduring, or even significant, values."* Do you agree with the quotation? Discuss, supporting your position with examples from current affairs, literature, history, or your own experience. In your discussion be sure to make clear what you consider a hero to be.

3. *"Outrageous behavior is instructive. It reveals to us the limits of our tolerance."* The quotation implies that those who go beyond accepted standards help us to clarify our own standards. Do you agree or disagree with the quotation? Discuss, supporting your position with examples from current affairs, literature, history, or your own experience.

4. *"Human beings make mistakes, but they also have great moments. One of those great moments, in my opinion, was _____."* Complete this statement with an example from literature, history, current affairs, or your own experience. Using the completed statement, write a well-organized essay in which you explain *why* you regard that moment in such a positive light.

Strategy Notes

Zero In. During the first two minutes of the test, reduce the prompt to a topic of one to three words. (In the case of "Any advance involves some loss," the topic might be "sacrifice" or "success demands sacrifice.")

Devise and Conquer. Pull together a plan of attack during the first two or three minutes of the exam that can illustrate your zeroed-in topic. Start with paragraph types. Do you start with a narrative anecdote that sets up and illustrates your topic? Do you describe in detail a particular behavior that illustrates your topic? The key here is to pick a very strong narrative or vividly descriptive example of the topic. Next, choose a thesis paragraph style that deals with the concept to be proven. The definition mode (see pages 139–141) utilizes several techniques that can reveal your technical prowess as a writer, from typical and specific example use to negative definitions, metaphors, similes, and personal definitions. Another option for paragraph two might be the example paragraph (see page 141) in which you use examples to illustrate your argument. Your third paragraph is the ethos paragraph. This is what the writer believes about the topic—your personal position in terms of the moral position. As stated previously, this is your summation to the jury.

Paraphrase the Prompt. Put the prompt in your own words as soon as you can. This will give you a sense of control and ownership of the essay topic and get you focused right away. Don't restate the prompt verbatim in the essay until the very end—if at all—and then use it only as if it were your own research quote that finishes the essay with panache.

All the Right Moves. Style is crucial in the *SAT II: Writing Test*. It's not a test that is focused on intense content. The scorers want to see a variety of writing techniques, such as a variation of paragraph structures, a sense of varied syntax, a good sense of the use of leads, a keen ear for tone and a point of view that has energy and character. As I tell my writing classes, good writers tell their stories with an actor's voice. We can hear a person with tastes and attitude telling the story when a

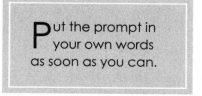

Put the prompt in your own words as soon as you can.

writer has the command of technique. We hear the writer speaking like a character in the piece. This essay test doesn't call for an omniscient narrator, so much as a character who knows what he or she is talking about and delivers the essay with color, action, meaning, and tone. That's style, plain and simple.

Mine Fields and Pitfalls Here are some important things to avoid as you write the *SAT II: Writing Test:*

• If the prompt asks "Do you agree or disagree?" with the quoted statement in the test, don't respond in the first paragraph with "I agree (or disagree) with the . . . blah, blah, blah." Ouch! This is doom in the exam. Please, just write an essay that is suggested by the prompt but never answer the prompt as if it were an essay "question." They want an essay—not an answer.

• Avoid religion or politics as topics. Both of these areas of discussion are about belief and belief is not a good territory for solid argument. Your opinions about religion or politics are only going to hurt your essay.

• Beware of the *You and I trap*. Don't use the second person in the essay and try to keep the first person to a minimum. Write about a topic, not about yourself. You can tell us about an experience, of course, but take care to avoid "I did this . . . and I think that . . . and I went there . . ."

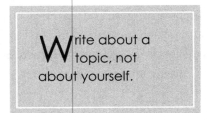

Write about a topic, not about yourself.

• You can't do everything so don't try to answer the prompt with an essay that discusses literature, history, science, current events, and your own perspective.

Less is more.

Celebrity Death Match. A quick way to destroy your score in the *SAT II: Writing Test* is to write about a celebrity for your topic. Don't discuss the hottest celebrity news item, regardless of how hot it is in the media. Believe me, that's what the horde of unimaginative writers at the time you are taking the test will do and you don't want to be with them on this topic choice. That means no mention of Dennis Rodman, J.F.K. Jr., Madonna, Puff Daddy and Jennifer, Britney, O.J., or whomever. Pop culture just isn't a good topic area for a serious exam. Go elsewhere for material.

9

The Graduate School Essay

Graduate school application essays are very similar in their requirements to college application essays. The objectives are the same. The essay is intended to give the admissions committee at graduate schools an idea of who you are. Graduate admissions officers very rarely interview applicants, and thus the essay is your only opportunity to sell yourself to the committee with a personal perspective. The graduate essay is a very important part of the application for the committee, perhaps more so than it is for undergraduates.

My advice to college seniors who are looking forward to graduate school or graduates in the working world readying themselves for the graduate school experience and are preparing their applications is to consider the essay to be equally important in value as college transcripts and standardized test scores. The reason the essay has such weight is that graduate schools are looking for diversity and special circumstances. As

> At the graduate level of admissions, the essay is the one chance you have to reveal the intangibles that aren't covered by your college grade point average and GRE scores.

one law school admissions office explained, "We don't want a class of geniuses. We want real people from varied backgrounds who will bring something special to the program." At the graduate level of admissions, the essay is the one chance you have to reveal the intangibles that aren't covered by your college grade point average and GRE scores.

The graduate admissions essay should focus on the following elements: leadership, experiences, goals, and special circumstances. These factors are not evident in your college transcripts and scores. They are, however, the areas that can bring you to life in ways that will lift you above the crowd of graduates vying for a place in law school, medical school, an MBA program, or a school of engineering.

Leadership

GRADUATE SCHOOLS are looking for leaders. One purpose of graduate school is to train people to manage, direct, and lead staffs and organizations. Management experience is an asset. Have you taken charge of a program or projects as an undergraduate? During your summers or years after college, have you undertaken any positions that can reflect your leadership qualities? If so, what did you learn about the experience? Has your leadership experience been related to your choice of graduate study? Were there any mentors under whose tutelage you learned significant points about management of crisis situations? Have you learned anything about the right way to deal with people? Such factors are key illustrations of your ability to lead. A topic for your essay can concentrate in part or wholly on this area of discussion. However, as this book indicates, just running down a list of leadership examples isn't nearly as effective as describing the details and nuances of the leadership roles you've enjoyed. Get personal. Tell the committee how you felt about the challenges and what they meant to you. How did being a leader make your goal more real and meaningful to you?

Experience

WHAT HAS happened to you in your life—before, during, and after college—that has shaped your drive, career choice, and ethical fabric? There is a place in your graduate school essay for this kind of discussion. A graduate school admissions officer told me, "We want to know about the person inside of the transcript . . . about their family and ethnic background. What kind of jobs they've had. Did they support their family with a full-time job? Did they work while they were in school? Did they do anything related to their career goal that shows they really want to make their mark in this field?"

At this point I suggest that you take another look at chapter 3. The exercises in that chapter are valuable for everyone who wants to write about experiences. Do the exercises completely. You will need all the information you can get to help you stand out from the thousands of students who are

> What has happened to you in your life—before, during, and after college—that has shaped your drive, career choice, and ethical fabric?

applying to the same school. The more detail from which you have to choose, the more special your experiences will seem. If any experiences have driven you to your choice of career and if any beliefs and models have influenced your choices, this is the time to discover what they are and make them come alive for the graduate admissions committee. Even though you may feel that you have a sense of what you want to say in your graduate essay, a good place to begin the writing process is completing the profiles in chapter 3 because they will open up your mind to the depth of experiences that you've had that might need inclusion in your essay but that you've overlooked in your stress to write this very "tough" piece.

Goals

PLEASE READ the section in chapter 3 on goals. It can tell you everything you need to know about the importance of describing your goals or understanding how they may be used in your essay. Obviously, at the graduate level your goals should have some connection to reality. If you have been pursuing a career goal for the last few years, describe this pursuit in explicit terms, but make it personal. What inspired you to choose these goals? What has your experience in the world and college done to shape these goals? Don't try to sound lofty or pretentious. Talk about your goals in your own words. Be yourself when you talk about your goals and the goals will sound real.

> Make the situation a positive attribute that reveals your character and resourcefulness.

My advisory work with graduate students over the last ten years has given me the opportunity to see a variety of essays that dealt with the discussion of goals. Certainly, the best essays were those that demonstrated a clear connection of past experiences, internships, work history, and study to the goals that each of my grad students were aspiring to achieve. The details, narrative and descriptive, that formed the basis of the long, arduous trek toward these goals were always told with a sense of the clear and determined purpose, however circuitous the path might seem, that drove the candidate toward that goal.

Special Circumstances

THE PHRASE "special circumstances" is a catchall euphemism for anything that might explain or shed light upon the performance of the candidate for admission. It offers permission to discuss areas of a student's personal background that should merit special consideration, such as economic background, international origins, physical handicaps, and traumatic experiences. Ethnicity is a special circumstance for some admissions committees because they have an affirmative action quota. Knowing if you are of a particular race might determine whether to waive certain negative factors in your folder. Were you raised by a single parent? Did you put yourself through college? Is English your second language? Are you a refugee from a war-torn nation? The graduate school admissions essay is the only place in the application wherein you can mention this type of information. How you mention it is crucial.

If you have special circumstances that should be considered, tell the committee about the details of your situation in a way that makes them come alive. Use imagery that makes your story real. Don't just declare that life was difficult because Mom had to work and was never there to raise your family. What feelings did you have about the circumstance? What did it teach you about life and yourself? If your special circumstance reads like an excuse, chances are that it won't be favorably received. Make the situation a positive attribute that reveals your character and resourcefulness.

Be Yourself

GRADUATE ADMISSIONS officers have told me to caution applicants to write the essay in a style that sounds like "who they are." Evidently they receive many essays that are written by students who try to sound "medical" or "legal" or "corporate," depending on the professional school to which they are applying. Nothing could be more counterproductive than to sound so artificial. *Be yourself.* Graduate schools are looking for people who know who they are, not people who are putting on an act. Write in your own words. The best way to prepare for this exercise is to tape your essay and then play it back to yourself a few days after you write it. If the essay still sounds like you, then it has achieved some degree of success: It is at least honest.

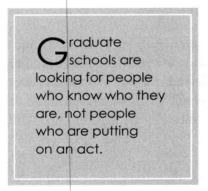

Graduate schools are looking for people who know who they are, not people who are putting on an act.

Final Advice

READ THIS book, cover to cover, before you write your essay. Everything written for undergraduate admission applies to the essay you will write. In most cases, your grad essay will be longer and demand more detail—all the more reason to read this book for attention to details that you may need to remember as you are writing this all important career opus.

Strategy Notes

Tell a Story. Somewhere in your essay you need to tell a story. Anecdotes are very successful devices in the graduate essay. They bring you to a three-dimensional status in the essay and show the admissions committee who you are or were. I've read essays that related stories of ancestors, on-the-job experiences, earliest childhood memories that connected the candidate to the career path, and every other kind of short narrative that made the otherwise dry substance of the essay resonate with life. It's a must.

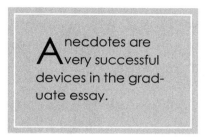

Anecdotes are very successful devices in the graduate essay.

Native Languages and Foreign Tongues. If you speak a language other than English, find a place somewhere in the essay to quote someone saying something in that language and then, of course, tell us what it means. Don't just say you speak Italian, or Spanish and Japanese, or whatever language—tell us a story or a saying in the language that demonstrates your ability in action. Plug it in to your essay and demonstrate your savvy without telling us again and again how much you love the culture.

Be True to Your School. Know the graduate school you are applying to and do the research it takes to sound like you really "checked them out" before applying. Be informed about who teaches there, what the program offers, the details about research libraries, discoveries or contributions to the line of work you're pursuing that have been made by faculty, opportunities that are available, and the history of the program. Let them know that you are a professional by doing what any pro does: Familiarize yourself with the terrain.

10

"It's Only Money!"

Writing Essays for Scholarships

M any colleges, universities, and scholarship foundations require an essay from any candidate who is being considered for or applying to the institution for a grant or scholarship. These essays are somewhat different from the personal statement that a student writes as part of the general application for admission. Often there are precise guidelines applied to a scholarship applicant's essay that have very different features from those for the personal statement that you wrote for admission to "Lucky U."

Check It Out

EVERY SCHOLARSHIP and grant is unique. This is an unspoken precept in the Law of Gifts. If you are applying for a particular scholarship (and there are thousands of scholarships and grants out there for students if they know where to look for them), then you should be aware of this precept. Never assume that one grant is like any other.

Scholarships are designed by individuals with individuals in mind. Scholarship committees follow the guidelines of individual donors in determining who can qualify for available grant money. Even in instances where corporations offer scholarship dollars to certain institutions, an individual perspective determined their criteria for the award. Every scholarship is focused on serving a particular kind of need, and therefore, it targets a particular kind of student. Often, eligibility is based on any number of factors, such as ethnic background, hardship, religion, family economic circumstances, veteran status of a family member, and even neighborhood. Also, not all scholarships are aimed at students with impeccable academic credentials. All are, however, aimed at students who have the ability to write an essay that declares a sincere need and desire for the scholarship in a convincing manner. This means that every scholarship should be looked at individually, with keen attention to the criteria of eligibility. The essay that you will be asked to write for a scholarship committee is the final element that will decide who gets the money. Before you ask this committee to consider giving you money for school, you should know something about these people and to whom they wish to give the money.

> The essay that you will be asked to write for a scholarship committee is the final element that will decide who gets the money.

Read about the scholarship foundations before you write the essays. Research is important here, because you have to tailor your essay to the requirements of the particular scholarship to which you apply. If need is a key factor in the criteria for the award and you are too proud to write about the fact that you and your family can't afford to pay for your college education, then you won't be awarded the scholarship. If the scholarship considers only specific ethnic criteria and you fail to feature your ethnic pride in your essay, then someone else who does so will win the scholarship.

Learn about the scholarship, and don't be afraid to ask questions if you don't think you know enough about it to write an essay. Too many students act too soon with too little knowledge when it comes to the college application and scholarship process. Before you write the essay, call the college or scholarship foundation and ask to speak to an assistant or director in the financial aid office or an officer in the department wherein the scholarship money is administered. You may have to wait on hold occasionally or find yourself in transit from one office to another, but don't give up until you speak with someone in authority. People will often be more than glad to explain to you the criteria that they use in determining the worthiness of a candidate, if you ask the right questions. Remember, these people are giving away money to students to help them go to college. That means they are often bogged down by paperwork late in the day, so call them in the morning. Don't be afraid to talk to them about your concerns, but be tactful and never demanding. They will want to help you if you are respectful and friendly, and especially if you ask polite questions that you have prepared in advance. An old Yiddish proverb says, "If you don't ask, you don't get."

> People will often be more than glad to explain to you the criteria that they use in determining the worthiness of a candidate, if you ask the right questions.

Stories of Need and Desire

OFTEN, THE essay topics that are used for a scholarship essay are very direct and no-nonsense. It is rare to find an essay question from a scholarship committee or foundation that asks you to write on an esoteric topic. These people are interested in four fundamental aspects of your background: your need, your desire, your ability, and your eligibility. Your essay should address each of these important concerns in some way.

Need

Today, it is a gargantuan task to put someone through college for any length of time. The need for scholarship money is increasing at a staggering rate, and so the competition for grants is heating up at every level of college admissions. Scholarship committees attempt to serve those in need. The very idea of scholarships based on need is one of the more civilized aspects of our democracy. Your essay may never mention this fact, but you should appreciate the remarkable contribution to freedom of thought that a scholarship represents before you begin to write your essay.

Essentially, the scholarship essay is most often a narrative that describes a certain set of aspects of your life. It should read like a story about a personal experience to be most effective. Instead of concentrating on interesting aspects of your personal perspective on life and learning, as is often the best course in the personal statement of your college application, the scholarship essay or "letter" (as it is sometimes called) should tell a story of you and/or your family's struggle to overcome difficult circumstances, your goals and the path you've taken to reach them, the value of education to you throughout this struggle, and the important role that a scholarship will play in helping you to realize your goals. Details, examples, and explanations of your need are absolutely necessary in this kind of essay. The element of need is a stage that must be set early in the essay.

Desire

Always a key factor in any contest, desire often determines the outcome of issues great and small. Your essay for scholarship consideration should demonstrate the degree of dedication to your education and goals that is reflected in your day-to-day living and working. This is also best portrayed in a narrative mode of expression. Don't give your résumé or a litany of your jobs. Tell us in story form about some of the jobs, activities, and responsibilities that you have embraced in order to fulfill your goals.

Ability

A sense of pride in your accomplishments is often easier to feel than to discuss in an essay. The most difficult feature of a scholarship essay for some students can be the part that may ask you to discuss your successes. The thought of declaring in words that you are a big fan of yourself often has the uncomfortable feel of immodest "bragging," and most people are somewhat ill at ease about "strutting their stuff" so openly in an essay. It's a normal reaction,

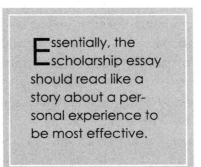

Essentially, the scholarship essay should read like a story about a personal experience to be most effective.

and there are ways of approaching your successes in this essay so that you don't come off as an egomaniac. First, discuss your successes in terms of what they have taught you about yourself and life. If they have kept the desire to learn alive in your heart throughout your struggles, then you need not feel badly in describing your successes. Remember, as in all essays for college applications, the most important aspect of any topic about which you write is the significance of what you do, think, or feel. Always *tell* the readers what value or meaning any experience has for you. Perhaps your successes have taught you the value of hard work or persistence. There is a place in your scholarship

> **B**abe Ruth once said, "It ain't braggin' if it's true."

essay for a brief discussion of this aspect of your accomplishments. Though Babe Ruth once said, "It ain't braggin' if it's true," the truth of your deeds will be spoken best by mention of their value to you as learning experiences.

Eligibility

The research that you do on the scholarships for which you are applying will yield an impressive list of specific criteria that applicants are required to meet. Make sure your essay mentions you in light of these criteria, and in a positive way, however subtle that mention might be. If you are an African-American or a Hispanic, for example, and minority status is called for in the scholarship criteria, mention your ethnic background in some way. You don't have to constantly reiterate your ethnic status in the essay; just include it in some way that identifies you with those who are eligible for the grant. Neglecting to mention important criteria that is specific to a certain type of grant is a mistake that doesn't seem like it would be so crucial, but when the committee that awards the money is adding up the data, your written account will often stand out much more dramatically than a box that you checked on the application that indicates you're eligible for the scholarship. Essays can have memorable impact in marketing you, but only robots care about boxes with check marks in them. Make sure your essay touches all the important bases.

11

Final Touches

A Brief Checklist

YOU'VE ASSEMBLED your essay paragraphs and decided on the five basic things you want to communicate to the admissions committee about *you*. If the essay is not a purely personal statement that will allow you complete control of the format, then you've decided what elements in your profile can be used in answering the freak essay question. You've read the sample essays in chapter 7 and have an idea of what you can do and what you should avoid. Here are some things that you want to make sure you do before you send your final draft.

1. Type the essay.

2. Check each paragraph for solid leads and clear topic sentences.

3. Sound-test the essay *before* you type the last draft to ensure that it sounds like you and not someone who's trying to sound like a pretentious intellectual.

4. Check each paragraph to see if it ends with a solid tag sentence.

5. Number each sentence in every paragraph, using the 3-2-1 scale for pacing to check the "sound" of your sentences.

6. Circle the first and last word of each sentence to see if you are repeating your beginnings and endings.

7. Circle every pronoun and then determine if it is absolutely clear that the reader will know what the *it, them, him* or *her,* and *they* actually refer to without having to read back more than a few phrases or one sentence.

8. Make sure you didn't try to say too much or tell your complete life story.

9. Be sure the essay is about *you.* If it's about someone else or an idea that doesn't relate to your experience, trash it and start over.

10. Have your editor read the essay and check it for spelling and punctuation *before* you type the final draft.

11. Make sure each sentence follows logically from the sentence before it. Look for gaps in your flow and fill them if you find them.

12. Read chapter 5 one more time and check your essay with it in hand, point by point.

13. Reread chapter 7. Are you doing the right thing or making the same mistakes that are bad and ugly? Change what needs to be changed, or congratulate yourself if it reads well.

14. Be sure every paragraph is keeping you and your experience and ideas center stage.

15. Check that feeling and emotion are in your essay. Are you letting your humanity show?

16. Be sure there are visual illustrations in each paragraph.

17. If you're trying to be funny, have you tried your essay on a stranger who doesn't know you? If he or she doesn't laugh, neither will the admissions officers.

18. Now type the final draft.

19. Double-space it.

20. Indent the paragraphs.

21. Make sure you have generous horizontal and vertical margins.

22. Use clean, white paper.

23. Don't use white-out. Keep the copy clean. Have a professional typist do your last draft if you can't type well.

24. Put your first and last name on each page.

25. Number the pages.

26. Don't write more than 500 words or two pages.

27. Title the essay at the top of page 1.

28. Ask your editor to proofread the essay one last time.

29. Make sure the address on the application envelope and the college for which you're writing the essay are one and the same.

30. Make sure that the pages are together in correct sequence.

31. Put the essay into the envelope with your application, checking to see if you wrote in the space on the application where the essay is supposed to fit (but never can): "See Attached Essay."

32. Seal the essay in the envelope only when you know that you've made two extra copies of everything in the application just in case it doesn't get to "Lucky U." due to a mailing mystery.

33. Mail the whole package ahead of the deadline at the post office. Don't trust the local street pickup box. Have the post office weigh the envelope and send it out via first class mail.

34. Breathe a sigh of relief and know that you did your best. Congratulations.

35. Buy a small gift or thank-you card for your mentor.

36. Pray. It can't hurt.

BIBLIOGRAPHY

This bibliography is a collection of suggested references for your essay writing. The dictionaries and etymologies may help you find a direction in which to write when you are unsure of the meaning of a concept or need some stimulus to move your essay in a fresh direction. The collection of quotation references may also help to inspire you in the quest to say what you mean, as you read what others have said about similar themes. There are some marvelous and important ideas about life and learning in these books—even though the titles on the covers may not sound very exciting. Take a look at a few of these sources as you write your essay.

Dictionaries

DeVinne, Pamela, ed. *American Heritage Illustrated Encyclopedic Dictionary.* Boston: Houghton Mifflin, 1982.

Flexner, Stuart Berg, ed. *The Random House Dictionary of the English Language.* New York: Random House, 1987.

Gove, Phillip B., ed. *Webster's Third New International Dictionary Unabridged.* New York: G. & C. Merriam, 1976.

Murray, A. H. et al., eds. *The Oxford English Dictionary.* 13 vols. Oxford: Clarendon Press, 1961.

Etymology

Barnhart, Robert K., ed. *The Barnhart Dictionary of Etymology.* W. Wilson, 1988.

Ciardi, John. *Good Words to You.* New York: Harper & Row, 1987.

Collinge, N.E. *An Encyclopedia of Language.* 2 vols. New York: Routledge, 1989.

1811 Dictionary of the Vulgar Tongue. London: Bibliophile Books, 1984.

LeMay, H.; Lerner, S.; and Taylor, M. *New Words.* New York: Facts on File, 1988.

Morris, M., and Morris, W. *Dictionary of Word and Phrase Origins.* 2 vols. New York: Harper & Row, 1967.

Murray, Sir James Augustus Henry. *New English Dictionary of Historical Principles.* 10 vols. and supplement. Oxford: Clarendon Press, 1888-1933.

Onions, C.T., ed. *The Oxford Dictionary of English Etymology.* Oxford: Clarendon Press, 1966.

Shipley, Joseph T. *The Origin of English Words.* Baltimore: Johns Hopkins University Press, 1984.

Quotations

Benham, Sir William Gurney. *Benham's Book of Quotations, Proverbs and Household Words.* New York: Putnam's, 1949.

Brussel, Eugene E. *Dictionary of Quotable Definitions.* Englewood Cliffs, N.J.: Prentice-Hall, 1970.

King, Anita, comp. and ed. *Quotations in Black.* Westport, Conn.: Greenwood Press, 1981.

Magill, Frank N., ed. *Magill's Quotations in Context.* 2 vols. New York: Salem Press, 1965.

Morley, C., ed. *Familiar Quotations in Context.* 2 vols. New York: Salem Press. 1965.

Oxford Dictionary of Quotations. New York: Oxford University Press, 1986.

Partnow, Elaine, comp. and ed. *The Quotable Woman, 1800-1981.* New York: Facts on File, 1982.

Roberts, Kate Louise, ed. *Hoyt's New Cyclopedia of Practical Quotations.* New York: Funk and Wagnall, 1964.

INDEX